Our Hope for Years to Come
The Valparaiso University Prayer Book

editors
Gail McGrew Eifrig
Frederick Niedner

Acknowledgements:

Collects from *Lutheran Book of Worship* (LBW) © 1978 by permission of Augsburg Fortress. p. 12, 14, 16, 36, 38, 40, 42, 62, 88, 90, 109, 110, 112, 114, 116, 118, 120, 122, 123, 162.

Hymns © 1978 *Lutheran Book of Worship* (LBW). Reprinted by permission of Augsburg Fortress. p. 13, 15, 17, 61, 72, 91, 120, 122, 127, 146.

Excerpt from "A Christmas Hymn" from *Advice to a Prophet and Other Poems*. © 1961 and renewed 1989 by Richard Wilbur, reprinted by permission of Harcourt, Inc. p. 63.

Collects from *Lutheran Worship* (LW) © 1982 Concordia Publishing House. Used with permission. p. 78, 80, 82, 84, 126, 168.

Norman Nagel, Dean of the Chapel of the Resurrection from 1968 to 1983, for Epiphany 1979. p. 103

Taken from RELIVING THE PASSION by WALTER WANGERIN, JR. © 1992 by Walter Wangerin, Jr. Used by permission of Zondervan Publishing House. p. 138.

Bob Springsteen for use of material by Anne Zink Springsteen. p. 155, 190, 194.

Setting from *Lutheran Worship* (LW) © 1980 Concordia Publishing House. Used with permission. p. 169.

From *Off-Key Phrases* © 1968 Concordia Publishing House. Used with permission. p. 175.

Text from pp. 14-15 from RAGMAN AND OTHER CRIES OF FAITH, by WALTER J. WANGERIN. © 1984 by Walter Wangerin, Jr. Reprinted by permission of HarperCollins Publishing, Inc. p. 185-186.

ISBN 0-9712294-0-6

First printing, June, 2001
9,000 copies in print

Published by Valparaiso University

Table of Contents

Preface

Included among God's many gifts to His people is His invitation for us to pray to Him. He not only promises to hear our prayers, but He also pledges He will answer our petitions and intercessions.

This conviction of God's openness to the prayers of His people motivated some leaders on the Valparaiso University campus to propose the creation of this devotional resource. It caused others to decide to underwrite the cost of creating and publishing this book. Still others were moved to write the prayers and submit the devotional materials that have been included in this volume. A select few employed their organizational and editorial skills to oversee the completion and the printing of this book.

Even a superficial acquaintance with the content of the Bible usually includes the knowledge of how over the centuries God's people prayed to Him. Jesus, Himself, prayed regularly to the Father. At the request of some of His disciples, He taught them the words of the Lord's Prayer. A maturing faith encompasses a more comprehensive knowledge and appreciation of the power and place of prayer in the life of a believer.

It is the hope of everyone who was involved in producing this resource that the content of these pages will inspire devotional reflection, promote the practice of praying regularly, edify the faith, and contribute to the sense of well-being for all who use this book.

Thanks to God for the women of the Valparaiso University Guild for their sustaining gifts over the years, particularly for enabling the production and printing of this resource.

May the Lord bless your use of this prayer book.

Alan F. Harre, President
Pentecost 2001

How to use this book

The Valpo Prayer Book lends itself to a variety of devotional options. Hopefully, it will serve its many users as a helpful resource for personal devotions, either daily or occasional, for leading worship in various public settings, or perhaps within a family as student and parent delve into readings together.

The book centers upon seven seasons of the church year. Within each season there are four or five different devotional resources. Each section alone, or in combination, can enrich the reader. For example, some will find the seven "introductions" that open up the seasons of the church year to be particularly enlightening. Others will find the "weekly devotions" during Advent, Epiphany, and Lent to be enriching.

Laced throughout the seven seasons of the church year are numerous prayers. They can be found under the headings of "Celebrating Lives of Faith," which call to mind the contributions of remarkable church leaders through the ages, and "Prayers of the Season," which capture events, times, situations, and places in the life of Valpo students.

This book also offers its readers an opportunity to celebrate the "Special Days" of the church year like Reformation and Pentecost. While most of these days will be celebrated in the company of fellow believers on campus or in one's own congregation, twelve devotionals are offered as a supplement to these most sacred days.

For those seeking a more extensive reading, there are excerpts from 28 memorable homilies and sermons "From the Chapel," which are sprinkled through the seven seasons.

Those who use the various aspects of this book for private, daily devotions likely will wish to consult a daily lectionary (suggested readings for every day of the year) in order to establish a pattern of Bible reading. Resources for such devotional use, especially hymns, are located on page 200.

No doubt you will find uses for this prayer book that its editors have not imagined. However you use this book, our hope is that your life in Christ be nurtured and matured.

Introduction

In this prayer book Valparaiso University's mission to nurture and deepen the faith lives of all who come here takes a new form. In these pages, we have tried to gather something of that mission into words and images, to accompany the reader in daily life routines shaped by—or at least influenced by—a desire to walk with God. Of course there are dozens of ways to make that walk, as there are hundreds of prayer books to help Christian people live out their vocations. Here, we've shaped the walk according to the calendar, rhythms, celebrations, and observances of the academic year as we live out the larger and older patterns of the liturgical or Church year.

This seems to us more than just a useful technique. In fact, it puts into tangible form the twin ribbons of two calendars—the secular and the sacred—and weaves them together in much the same way that we live out life at Valparaiso University. We are—at the same moment—faithful people living in the disciplines of Advent's preparation for Christmas and members of a community anxiously preparing for final exams. Those who have moved away from a calendar shaped by first days of class and mid-terms grades nonetheless live within the ancient rhythms of Lent, Easter, and Pentecost, even as they cope with ends of the fiscal year, tax time, birthdays, and other temporal markers.

We all live in time; the question is, how do we mark its passage so that we keep ourselves alive to its real meaning? As we constructed this book, that is the question we kept uppermost. How does the light that Valparaiso University strives to uphold help us to see our way through the joys and confusions of everyday living? It is our hope that this Prayer Book will reflect that light onto your path.

GM$\mathcal{E}$
FAN

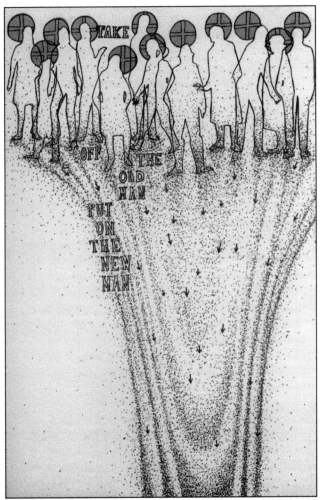

TAKE OFF THE OLD MAN PUT ON THE NEW MAN

Kuni Nuechterlein. October 1969

Michaelmas

The Season of Michaelmas

Unlike other prayer books, this one begins at a place that may surprise you—the beginning of the academic year, somewhere in late August or early September. In the Church calendar, that's deep into Pentecost, the season that started way back in May. We've adopted a traditional English name for the season, calling it after Michael, the heroic angel of great projects in God's name. After all, that's what we all intend when we start something—a school year, a new job, a project—to achieve something that will make the world better, improve our own lives, or in some other way, be about God's work in the world. In Christian legend, Michael fought off the devil, and in a hundred different ways, we are all about that work too, striving to combat evil in whatever form we meet it.

At Valpo, the beginning of the year brings with it introductions to worship at the Chapel of the Resurrection, that majestic structure where much of the campus religious life finds its center. New students sometimes find that they have to struggle to adapt themselves to the space itself, or to new ways of doing things. The Chapel is not only a physical structure; its role in the community also demands administrative structures, committees, routines, schedules—all components of a large institution. It has history and tradition, habits and routines, some of these rather mysterious, many of them subject to challenge and change as generations of worshipers move to its rhythms.

This Prayer Book, then, that would like to accompany you through a year of spiritual growth and devotion, begins as the school year begins at the Chapel. The academic community begins its life as hundreds of individuals gather to pledge themselves to a common calendar, a common purpose, and a common life, lived out in hundreds of different ways. The struggle to develop as an individual within community is the struggle that marks the beginning

of a school year, but that struggle also characterizes the

faith journey every Christian faces again and again. Each of us has a personal life, with its own needs, triumphs, griefs and joys. Yet, we do not live alone but within the great community of the Church throughout time. In this opening season of our year together, Michael stands as an emblem, both of our individual struggles and the victories of the gathered community of Christ.

In this first section, we have collected a number of prayers and readings that are relevant to a variety of occasions connected with beginnings, with some of the traditions of the Valpo year, and with great lives of faith commemorated during this time of the year—whether we call it end of Pentecost, Michaelmas, beginning of school, or, like the rest of our world, just "autumn."

Celebrating Lives of Faith

(the following usually fall during Michaelmas)

September 10
O. P. Kretzmann

"Most gracious Father, I remember before you this day your good and faithful servant, Otto Paul Kretzmann, under whose stewardship you transformed Valparaiso University from the dream of a few into the achievement of thousands who, through the twenty-eight years of his presidency, were moved by his courage, his eloquence, his vision, and his faith to offer themselves and their own gifts to your service. For our Lord Jesus Christ's sake. Amen."

John Strietelmeier

September 18
Dag Hammarskjold: Peacemaker, 1961

Almighty God, you are Lord of the nations, beyond politics, beyond favorites. All people are your children. Thank you for the life of your servant Dag, who gave his life to help the United Nations become a viable instrument for human peace. Though he knew the UN's value, he also knew its weakness, and he placed his trust for true peace in you. Help me to find the cause that fits my faith and to work for it fearlessly. Amen.

September 21
Saint Matthew, Gospel writer

On this day I give thanks for the life of the gospel writer Matthew, and for the inspiration that he worked to turn into words. Our lives as Christians would be much poorer without his perfect expressions, from his account of the Wise Men's questions to his detailed descriptions of the Passion. May we bring to all our endeavors Matthew's willingness to leave behind what is second-best and follow you alone. In Christ's name. Amen.

September 29
St Michael

When I know that I need strength, when I feel like giving up, when I am feeling really breakable and alone, remind me that in your grace, Lord God, you have allowed us to know angels. Even though their existence is mysterious to us, we sometimes experience their presence, gving comfort, strength, and support. Michael's powerful opposition to evil is both an example and an incentive to me when I back away from a struggle I should be part of. Thank you for angels, in whatever form I see them. Amen.

October 4
St. Francis of Assisi

Lord, many things surround me, and I can't imagine being without them all. As I remember your servant St. Francis today, I am reminded that he literally gave up everything he had to follow you. Help me to think less of my earthly possessions that I might possess with greater devotion the joy also of following you. For Christ Jesus' sake.Amen.

October 18
St. Luke, Evangelist

Healing God, physician of body and soul, I give thanks to you this day for your servant Luke who wrote of the love and healing power of your Son. Renew in me Luke's concern for the poor, the outcast, and all in need of your healing touch. Continue through your body the Church the power to love and heal through Jesus Christ our Lord. We pray in Christ's name. Amen.

October 23
St. James of Jerusalem, brother of our Lord

Lord of the Church, your servant James provided leadership at a time when believers were just beginning to sense your vision for the world. I thank you this day for the example of James who endured hardship and ridicule in order that the reconciling power of your love might be spread throughout Jerusalem to the ends of the earth. In Christ's name. Amen.

October 26
Philipp Nicolai (1608)' Johann Heermann (1647), Paul Gerhardt (1676), Hymnwriters

"Thank you, Lord God, for the lives of your servants Philipp Nicolai, Johann Heerman, and Paul Gerhardt. Even as they witnessed the scourges of war, sickness, and deprivation, they bore witness all the more steadfastly to your boundless love through hymns of thanksgiving, meditation, and praise. I thank you for the glorious gift of song, remembering that it is both my duty and my joy to return it to you. Amen."

Peter Mercer-Taylor

November 11
Soren Kierkegaard, father of
Modern Existentialism

Gracious God of all that is noble and true. In his quest to renew the spirit of the Church to one that celebrated a full awareness of our existence in Christ, your servant Soren Kierkegaard suffered brutal rejection. I thank you for his courage in the risks of life and faith to teach us the vastness of your truth made known in the Word made flesh, Jesus Christ my Lord. Amen.

November 25
Isaac Watts

You who gave a new song to sing, Jesus my Lord, I give thanks to you this day for the life of your servant Isaac Watts. Through him you provided a voice with which to praise your wondrous works and sing of your glory. Thank you for his skillful art that continues to offer timeless expression of my faith in you, Jesus Christ my Savior. Amen.

Special Days

September 14
Holy Cross Day

Collect from *LBW*: "Almighty God, your son Jesus Christ was lifted high upon the cross so that He might draw the whole world to Himself. Grant that we who glory in His death for our salvation may also glory in His call to take up our cross and follow Him; through your Son, Jesus Christ our Lord, who lives and reigns with you and the Holy Spirit, one God, now and forever. Amen."

reading: John 12:20-33. "Whoever loves his life will lose it...."

Meditation

The cross is one of the strangest religious symbols imaginable. But it stands at the center of our faith's deepest truths: only in this death has evil finally been overturned. Only here, as Jesus becomes the victim, has all victimizing been shown up for what it is—the deep desire for destruction of everything, even of God. But Jesus as scapegoat revises the usual pattern of victimization, even the usual pattern of sacrifice. In Jesus' death, the old vicious habits are revealed. No longer can humans kill off a victim and say, "We're now all right; the evil one in our midst has been killed." Instead, this victim, God's own self, signals a new dynamic. God remains the ultimate giver and forgiver, not the angry deity placated by sacrifice, but the overturner of our entire trust in sacrifice itself.

It is the greatest mystery of the faith—the death of our human addiction to victimization as the way to please God. As the statue above the altar in the Chapel of the Resurrection affirms, Christ the King does not abandon His cross but forever uses it as His vehicle, His springboard and launching pad for all the world to see. All Christian thought comes again and again to this puzzle of the cross, and recognizes here both its deep truth and its deep mystery. On this day, Christians pause to wonder together at God's unfathomable love for human beings, expressed through those creatures' own peculiar instrument of torture and death.

Hymn Stanza

WERE YOU THERE WHEN THEY NAILED HIM TO THE TREE?
WERE YOU THERE WHEN THEY NAILED HIM TO THE TREE?
OH, SOMETIMES, IT CAUSES ME TO TREMBLE!—TREMBLE!—
TREMBLE!
WERE YOU THERE, WHEN THEY NAILED HIM TO THE TREE?

(LBW #92)

Closing Prayer

Lord God, before the mystery of the crucifixion, and before the sight of the Cross as the vehicle of the victorious Christ's presence, I confess that I am baffled and silent. I do not understand just how this terrible instrument of suffering can be an object of glory. But I trust in your promise that it is so, and that its mystery carries my salvation. Help me, even when I do not understand. Amen.

October 31

Reformation Day

Collect from *LBW*: "Almighty God, gracious Lord, pour out your Holy Spirit upon your faithful people. Keep them steadfast in your Word, protect and comfort them in all temptations, defend them against all their enemies, and bestow on the Church your saving peace; through your Son, Jesus Christ our Lord, who lives and reigns with you and the Holy Spirit, one God, now and forever. Amen."

reading: Psalm 46. "God is our refuge and strength...."

Meditation

Humans have a tendency to focus on heroes, and in celebrating Reformation, those Christians who are Lutheran always have turned to Luther as though he were a superhero. But we forget that his own preference was not to be the center of attention in the struggle to reform the Church. Probably he would be happier if his efforts to bring back into the Church the prime position of the Bible had done just that—and not resulted in something called a "denomination" at all, much less with his name attached to it. He wanted the focus to remain on Christ.

Today, all Christians engage constantly in reformation—starting from within. Our hearts re-form into instruments of love and mercy, we re-form the world of which we are a part, constantly trying to overcome fear and lying and oppression with this word from Jesus as Lord of the Church: Come to God, your Father, who loves you and wants only good for you. With that reformation, all Christians are "heirs of the Reformation," workers with Christ, with Luther, with all who love the Church, to shape the world towards God's design.

Hymn Stanzas

A MIGHTY FORTRESS IS OUR GOD, A SWORD AND SHIELD
VICTORIOUS;
HE BREAKS THE CRUEL OPPRESSOR'S ROD AND WINS
SALVATION GLORIOUS.
THE OLD, EVIL FOE, SWORN TO WORK US WOE; WITH
DREAD CRAFT AND MIGHT
HE ARMS HIMSELF TO FIGHT; ON EARTH HE HAS NO
EQUAL.

NO STRENGTH OF OURS CAN MATCH HIS MIGHT, WE
WOULD BE LOST, REJECTED.
BUT NOW A CHAMPION COMES TO FIGHT, WHOM GOD
HIMSELF ELECTED.
ASK WHO THIS MAY BE: LORD OF HOSTS IS HE! JESUS
CHRIST, OUR LORD,
GOD'S ONLY SON, ADORED. HE HOLDS THE FIELD
VICTORIOUS.

(LBW #228)

Closing Prayer

Lord God, you promised to love your Church through all
time. Give those who are responsible for churches today
the courage to be faithful to your word. Help me to have
patience and love for all the Church as for the Body of
Christ, to work to heal the separations and divisions within
it, and to care passionately for its welfare. In Christ Jesus'
name and for His sake. Amen.

November 1
All Saints Day

Collect from *LBW*: "Almighty God, whose people are knit together in one Holy Church, the Body of Christ our Lord: Grant us grace to follow your blessed saints in lives of faith and commitment, and to know the inexpressible joys you have prepared for those who love you; through your Son, Jesus Christ our Lord, who lives and reigns with you and the Holy Spirit, now and forever. Amen."

reading: Matthew 5:1-12. "...blessed are the pure in heart, for they shall see God."

Meditation

These words of Jesus inevitably make us feel humbled: how many of us would admit that we are poor in spirit, mourning, meek, hungering for righteousness, merciful, pure in heart? These are not the qualities that we would want to see on our resumes. Yet these are the qualities of persons Jesus called "blessed" and the qualities of those we recognize on All Saints' Day. These are the heroes of our faith, the ones who get Jesus' own seal of approval.

Should we stay with our feelings of unworthiness? yes and no. Even these saints were, at the same time, sinners, too. Yet their saintliness was based in the same place as our own saintliness—in the redemptive love and sacrifice Jesus made for us all. As Christian people, we celebrate All Saints' Day as both an honor to those great ones of the faith, and as a reminder to ourselves that all of us—saints and sinners—are at one and the same time saint and sinner. All of us have a place before God through God's own actions on our behalf. This is worth celebrating!

Hymn Stanzas

FOR ALL THE SAINTS WHO FROM THEIR LABORS REST
ALL WHO BY FAITH BEFORE THE WORLD CONFESSED
YOUR NAME, OH JESUS, BE FOREVER BLEST.
ALLELUIA! ALLELUIA!

OH, BLEST COMMUNION, FELLOWSHIP DIVINE,
WE FEEBLY STRUGGLE, THEY IN GLORY SHINE;
YET ALL ARE ONE, WITHIN YOUR GREAT DESIGN.
ALLELUIA! ALLELUIA!

(LBW #174)

Closing Prayer

Lord, let me come into your presence today fully aware of
my place as only one among many. Give me openness to
the greatness of others, to the gifts and talents in
Christian living that are examples to me. Make your
Church a place where saints are recognized and nurtured,
whatever their status in the world. For Christ's sake.
Amen.

Prayers of the Season

Opening Convocation Hymn

O GOD, OUR HELP IN AGES PAST,
OUR HOPE FOR YEARS TO COME,
OUR SHELTER FROM THE STORMY BLAST,
AND OUR ETERNAL HOME:

UNDER THE SHADOW OF YOUR THRONE,
YOUR SAINTS HAVE DWELT SECURE:
SUFFICIENT IS YOUR ARM ALONE,
AND OUR DEFENSE IS SURE.

BEFORE THE HILLS IN ORDER STOOD,
OR EARTH RECEIVED ITS FRAME,
FROM EVERLASTING YOU ARE GOD,
TO ENDLESS YEARS THE SAME.

A THOUSAND AGES IN YOUR SIGHT
ARE LIKE AN EVENING GONE,
SHORT AS THE WATCH THAT ENDS THE NIGHT,
BEFORE THE RISING SUN.

TIME, LIKE AN EVER-ROLLING STREAM,
SOON BEARS US ALL AWAY;
WE FLY FORGOTTEN, AS A DREAM
DIES AT THE OP'NING DAY.

O GOD, OUR HELP IN AGES PAST,
OUR HOPE FOR YEARS TO COME,
STILL BE OUR GUARD WHILE TROUBLES LAST
AND OUR ETERNAL HOME!

(LBW #320 text by Isaac Watts, 1674-1748)

A prayer for students

Grant, O Lord, to all students, to know what is worth knowing, to love what is worth loving, to praise what delights you most, to value what is precious in your sight and to reject what is evil in your eyes. Grant them true discernment to distinguish between different things. Above all, may they search out and do what is most pleasing to you; through Jesus Christ our Lord. Amen.

Thomas à Kempis

Beginning of a new school year

Lord God, you began the creation of the world with your vital word. Your human creation seeks to model your creating spirit every time we begin some new thing. Here at the beginning of a new school year, give us energy to sustain what we undertake today with excitement and good intentions. Help us to see ourselves as one community, and to remember—in the middle of all our individual hopes and projects—the common good of all as we strive to live in your light. In Christ's name. Amen.

For those back home

It feels more and more, God, as if I have two homes, and the one I still call "home" is the one where I spend the least time. Yes, Lord, this campus is becoming another home, and when I'm here I easily lose touch with all the ones I love "back home." Keep them in your care. Sustain them in their struggles. Hold them together with each other in your love, and me with them. Lead us to discover new and wonderful ways to be family with each other as these years unfold. Amen.

For Guild convention

"Thank you, God, for our Past: for the history of this University and the VU Guild; for baptism, memories, friendships, and especially for the life and death and resurrection of Jesus Christ. Thank you, God, for our Present: for this day, with its beauty and promise, this year with its camaraderie and sharing, and for the reality of the Body of Christ. Thank you, God, for our Future: for the challenges ahead, the expectation of reunions to come, the opportunity to use our talents wherever you lead us, and for the gifts of the Spirit. You give us all that we have, and all that we are, and you give us all to one another. Thank you, God, for everything. In Jesus' name we pray. Amen."

Fall weather

This week has been so beautiful, Lord, that every time I look around, I feel that I should call out to everybody, "Look at that tree! Look at that tree!" Of course, I'd be a total idiot to do it, but I just want you to know that at least one person has noticed. All around campus the colors sing and shout with reds and yellows, and the slopes of the little hills to the southwest show off the gentle molding of a countryside that is running over with beauty. Thank you for these days of fall's blue skies and sunshine, for the light and color that make each day seem like a special blessing. Amen.

Choosing a major

Lord God, you are the one I count on to know me better than anyone—better than my parents, better than my best friend. Won't you give me some clear sign about what I should plan to do with my life? Here at the University, people are always talking about vocation, but I don't hear any call, not yet anyway. There are things I like to do, and there are things I'm good at, but none of these seem to me to say "Career" in any powerful way. As this year gets going, I feel more and more pressure to get into some slot so that I can move along with a plan, but I still feel clueless. Where can I be the person I need to be? Amen.

Homecoming

Lord God, you created the idea of home, and from the first moments in the Garden of Eden, you made humans desire it. When we call our University an "alma mater," we name that constant desire to find a mother of our spirit, the homemaker who calls us to a place where we are known and cherished. Give Valparaiso University the grace to continue to make such a home for her graduates, so that they return here, drawn not only to the pleasure of good times, but also by their sense that here they have come closer to knowing you. Amen.

Mid-semester break

First let me take a deep breath, God. There, that's better. We've made it—at least to the half-way point. Yes, there is that second half of the semester still ahead, but this is a milestone. I've known your sustaining presence this far. I know you will be with me the rest of the way. Bless the work I have accomplished and let it flower and unfold in the weeks ahead. But now, for a moment, just bless this deep breath. Amen.

Having a vocation

Again today I felt it, walking down the corridor to the classroom of my favorite class—Yes! this is it, this is where I belong! I can't wait to know more, to become more competent, to find myself more and more talking about the things that really get me excited. Somehow everything is fitting together, and when my prof told me that I've done really well, it just seemed to me that my life took on more meaning and purpose than it's ever had before. Keep with me, Lord, and direct me as I move forward with this. Amen.

Thanksgiving

YES! A whole week break! And I have so many things saved up to do I will never get around to them all. I must find time to catch up on reading for class and start that paper. Then there's my family and friends—I want time with them. I'll want to help with Thanksgiving Day. Christmas shopping. Sorry, God, I'm having trouble focusing. Thank you for all of the above and for everything else on my Big List. Let me receive them all as gifts from you, and on top of it all grant me a grateful heart. Amen.

Opening of a sport's season

Nobody ever mentions sports in the Bible, Lord, but if we're supposed to pray without ceasing, I think that could involve our team's season. Give the players the season they hope for: good wins, no injuries, post-season play. Give the coaches and trainers wisdom and patience. Help us all to know sports as a way to use our best gifts as human creatures, enjoying strength, laughter and excitement. Let Valpo be known for all that is best in college athletics, and let me be part of that best. Amen.

From the Chapel

"The Angels of Michael"

"However, there is one distinctive kind of satanic destruction and harassment which Christians, and Christians alone, are equipped to deal with. St. John refers to this when he calls the Devil "the accuser," who day and night accuses the brethren. It is by his accusations, more than anything else, that Satan succeeds, as John says, in deceiving the whole world. And of what crime does he accuse the brethren? He accuses them of sin. But aren't they sinful? Indeed they are, mortally sinful. But by his accusations of sin, he deceives them into believing that God is angry with them and that God demands their death. But God is angry with them and He does demand their death. Yes, but the Devil by his accusations deceives men into thinking that God is only angry with them, that God wills nothing but their death, that there is no alternative to their sinfulness—unless they themselves can devise some way to appease this angered God, unless they themselves can by some moral and religious exertion justify their own existences. This is where the Devil is most shrewd, most effective—not in the laboratories but in the churches, not in men's sciences but in their religion. By his insidious accusations—persuasive because they are always more than half true—he can turn a man into a Pharisee or into a Judas. It is because of his accusations that Christians go about with long faces, gossipers and grumblers, unwilling to believe with their hearts what they confess with their lips: that by the mercies of Christ we are as righteous and alive as He is. How effectively the old Dragon has prevented us from believing that. The Devil knows well that, if by the diversionary tactic of his accusation he can separate the Christian angels from their faith and confidence and hope, then he will have separated them from their faith's Lord, from their only source of strength.

"But it is precisely at this vulnerable point, isn't it, that our Lord has overcome the Dragon. The shining Son of God, the express image of the Father, has assumed not only our flesh but our sin and our curse, and has submitted in our stead to the terrible accuser. And in accusing this holy One of God, the Devil has over-extended himself, and stands judged by his own condemnation. Hence, St. John can say, with magnificent and holy humor, that the terrible, cosmic, thundering powers of darkness have been overcome, and by what? By the blood of a Lamb—and from henceforth, by the testimony of His Word.

"For the scientist whose robes—even his lab coat!—have been washed by the blood of this Lamb, there is joy and courage and assured hope. He knows, of course, that viruses and coronaries and malignancies not only can be nuisances; they can be heretics, sent into the lives of men to rob them of their faith, and, eventually, rob them of their Lord. He knows, too, that often thorns and thistles are the long finger of the Accuser, sent to dampen men's spirits and to crush their souls. But, more important, he knows that the Accuser has already been routed and put to flight, that the issue of the battle has been decided, that the skirmish which remains is just the mopping up, that the appropriate attitude for himself—as for every angel of Michael—is to rejoice and to exult:

> "ASK YE, WHO IS THIS? JESUS CHRIST IT IS,
> AND THERE'S NONE OTHER GOD.
> HE HOLDS THE FIELD FOREVER."

Robert W. Bertram
excerpted from The Cresset, September 1958, pp. 12-14.

The Economy of Forgiveness

"The 'Personals' section of our newspaper recently carried this item: 'SCOTT Please come home or call. We love you. MOM & DAD.' If Scott listens, these parents have gained their son. If not, he stays lost.

"Behind all such losses is one who sins against another. A 'family' falls into 'commercial' or 'legal' relationships as Debtors and Creditors. First, you lose your brother. Then, by some cosmic order, you don't just end up with nothing, but a debtor replaces the brother. Even that wouldn't be so bad if we didn't make such a 'big deal' out of it.

I'm OK. You're OK. God Covers Our IOUs

"We chronically do exactly that, however. We cling to debtor/creditor relationships and hold others there. This applies not only to the creditors who hold debtors ('You did me wrong, and I want my pound of flesh!'), but also to debtors who have a perverse love/hate ambivalence about their debtor situation. We persist in debtor/creditor relationships because they offer the tempting promise of saving our lives. As a creditor, getting my pound of flesh allows me to save face, self-esteem, and finally my life. The permanent debtor mirrors the creditor, for permanent debt guarantees constant attention from my creditor. If she hates me, she at least pays attention to me. I count. I'm worth someone's attention. I even get a part of her life in this deficit accounting game. Through my indebtedness, I control her. She's not 'free' of me.

"Sisters and brothers remain lost amidst these bookkeeping transactions by which we seek to save ourselves. We lose each other, and finally ourselves.

"Jesus offers new insight into this problem by upsetting the ledger books we bank on. 'Whoever would save his life will lose it, and whoever loses his life for my sake will find it.' That's upsetting. Life is not a win-or-lose situation, nor does everybody win. Initially, we all lose. Thus, the central issue in the ledger of life is how you do your losing. Sinners cannot escape losing their lives. But in one way of losing life you gain life. Moreover, that life is full of brothers and free of debtors. It is the way of the cross.

"First the gospel breaks open the trap of our self-inflicted debtor/creditor salvation. God in Christ opens the cosmic trap by bearing in his body on the cross the debts of all whose accounts are so mortally overdrawn. On Easter morning with the opening of the tomb, he offers escape from the dead end of our debtor's prison. The good news of his death and resurrection provides an alternate source for gaining our lives. The data of old debits and credits remain, but we needn't try to gain our lives from them. Instead, we gain our lives by 'losing them for his sake.' How? By holding on to Christ in faith as he holds on to us. By trusting him when he takes our debtor's page and says, 'I'll sign for that.'

"When it comes to lost brothers like Scott, the second use of the gospel is to open the trap of our debtor/creditor relationships. How do you lose a debtor and gain a daughter or mother, a husband or wife, a brother or sister? You do as was done to you. You escape debtor status and become God's child, sibling of His only-begotten Son, by forgiveness.

"Forgiveness is the only way to restore families. Christ calls us to forgive when 'the brother sins against us.' Confront him 'between you and him alone.' Don't grab him by the neck and demand, 'Pay me what you owe!' Jesus' parable tells the deadly consequence—for the creditor!—of such confrontation.

"A Christian—the already-forgiven former debtor—brings the word of forgiveness into the conversation when the two of them get together. Only forgiveness has the power to 'gain' brothers. That is what the Creator created as the power for salvation. As God Himself well knows, forgiveness does not always work. Debtors and creditors can and do refuse to become sisters and brothers. Scotts do refuse to come home. But nothing else will work at all! That's the punch line in Jesus' counsel that if all attempts at forgiveness fail, 'let him be to you as a Gentile and a tax-collector.' Jesus did not write off such folks as bad debts. No, in his ledger they remain candidates for forgiveness, not really different from us who learn to pray 'forgive us our debts as we forgive our debtors'—daily.

"'Where two or three are gathered in my name, there am I in the midst of them.' This is the Lord's final promise that our forgiving is worth the risk. Why? Because He himself is on the scene when it transpires. The business we pursue is after all his business—and His Father's as well.

"Were it not for His pioneering such forgiveness economics with God's debtors in his body on the cross, we should have no light (and no right) to settle accounts except by debits and credits. That firstborn Son, our Brother, continues to pursue his business right 'in the midst' of us when two or three of us 'gather in His name.'

You Can Go Home Again, Scott, Free

"The ad for Scott appeared among the 'Personals.' It could just as well have been in the 'Lost and Found.' The gospel of forgiveness is God's way of going after lost people, and he commends it to us for finding our own lost ones. If Scott listens to their words of forgiving love, Mom and Dad gain their son. But forgiveness must happen— explicitly, concretely, palpably—to offset the debit/credit claims that will arise willy-nilly, else everybody stays lost. That is hard—a kind of death, no less—for us credit managers. The alternative is easier, though it means surer death and guaranteed loss. When we live by forgiveness, death becomes 'dying with the Lord,' losing 'for my sake and the gospel's.' It carries the heartening conclusion: 'you will gain your life . . . and your brother as well.' Amen."

Edward H. Schroeder
from The Cresset, January 1979, pp. 20-21

Valparaiso Hymn (often sung at Homecoming service)

"Valparaiso, Alma Mater"

> Valparaiso, Alma Mater,
> Gratefully we sing your praise.
> Flame of faith and lamp of learning
> Here have form'd our finest days.
> Thankful for your founders' vision,
> Others too in years to come
> Still will find on one fair campus
> Athens and Jerusalem.
>
> Father, you have in your image
> Form'd us handsomely endow'd.
> Send us out to probe your planets,
> Heal our neighbors, sway the crowd.
> Gospel freed from fear of knowledge,
> Let us spend our wit and might
> Learning, serving, feeding, feasting,
> For in your light we see light.

Philip Gehring

Gird Up your Minds

"God calls you to be holy. He calls you to be His own and His alone. The ground and content of that call are the offering of the precious Lamb, Jesus Christ, as the One by Whom you are God's.

"'You shall be holy for I am holy' is not only a demand; it is also a gift. It is the sacrifice for you. The great sacrifice will not be the one you make to train your minds in hard work. The great sacrifice is the one you receive.

"In that sacrifice, you will indeed make your own sacrifice. You will sit on your rumps, memorizing verb forms, formulae, tables, etc., even when you would prefer to be on the beach. You will practice, write and rewrite, training your minds to use words, precious words of human community and divine communication. But the sacrifice that hallows you and your mind is the one you receive, not the one you make.

"What is it then that makes for holy chemistry, mathematics, philosophy, art, psychology? It is that you are hallowed by the precious blood of Christ, the Lamb without blemish and without spot. As God's holy ones, that which you touch is hallowed as you are hallowed in the sacrifice of Christ Jesus.

"'Gird up your minds' then. Set your hope on that full pleasure of God toward you, that favor to be revealed in Christ Jesus at the end, as it has been revealed in Christ Jesus at the beginning. Walk in the fear of that God, the God of Truth. In His activity of 'truthing' you, may you learn to shun error, to pay the price of dispelling untruth, both in yourself and in the world.

"'You shall love the Lord your God with all . . . your mind.' What in goodness He demands of you, in graciousness He donates to you. Hear, hear indeed, His call to you to be holy, that the place of your vocation may be the sphere of your holiness."

Kenneth F. Korby 31
August 31, 1973

*From: The Inaugural Address
of Dr. Otto Paul Kretzmann
as President of Valparaiso University*
October 6, 1940
*Over the years, many Valparaiso University publications
have cited all or parts of Dr. O. P. Kretzmann's inaugural
address as the school's new president. These remarks on
October 6, 1940, just before the United States entered World
War II, spoke to that critical and difficult time in the
history of the nation and the University. As he concluded,
Dr. Kretzmann spoke specifically to the students in his
audience with the words that appear below.*

"If you will leave this campus prepared to become
thoughtful and intelligent citizens of a free and democratic
America; sympathetic and understanding healers of a torn
and broken society; great and courageous leaders of the
Body' of Christ in the world—then there is no power on
earth that can stop Valparaiso University in the attainment
of its destiny.

"In this spirit, then, I am deeply grateful for the privilege
of joining the company of men and women who have
prayed and worked for Valparaiso University these many
years. I know that our task is great. Our time is short. It is
later now than we think. We can not wait for another time
and another generation. Clearly aware of the magnitude of
our problems, deeply committed to the importance of our
work, humbly certain of our destiny, we may hope, under
God, to prepare a growing number of men and women who
will go out of this community into the darkness of a dying
world as the living embodiment of the motto of this
University, 'In Thy light we shall see light.' To that end I
implore the benediction of Almighty God."

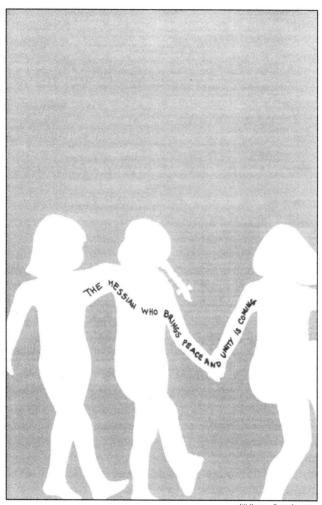

THE MESSIAH WHO BRINGS PEACE AND UNITY IS COMING

Jill Harper, December 1977

Advent

The Season of Advent

Advent marks the traditional beginning of the Church year, and yet for those in an academic community, it takes place during preparation for the end of the fall semester. And for those not in school, the time is characterized by the activities with which we bring a calendar year to a close. Clearly, too, the society in which we live is celebrating what we now call "the holidays," a confection of parties, occasions, gift-giving, and events that culminates on December 31. Christians who wish to remember the dynamics of Advent have their work cut out for them!

Perhaps you attend Sunday services at a church that marks the four Sundays of Advent with a wreath, or candles lit for the reading of special lessons foretelling the birth of the Savior. Perhaps you make such a wreath at home, or in your residence hall, or make a special effort at devotions for these weeks. Maybe you have an Advent Calendar, and look forward to opening each day's little window, whether you do this alone or with others in your circle. Think of this Prayer Book's moments of Bible reading and prayer as "little windows," through which all of us try to perceive the central truths of Advent: time is given to us by a loving God so that we can move toward Him; every person's time has a limit; in God's time, Jesus came to the world as a person to make clear how complete God's love for us really is; in God's time, Jesus will return to bring all time to a close.

Seeing these truths need not prevent us from enjoying all the Christmas preparations and holiday events. We will all put energy and excitement into the parties and concerts and shopping and cooking, just as those of us in school put energy into completing papers and studying for exams.

Most people who have attended Valpo keep a special place in their hearts for the thrilling beauty of the traditional

Advent-Christmas Vespers. But Christians always will see these things as part of a whole, as reflections of deep human desires and needs that are only partially fulfilled in the activities we eagerly design and carry out.

This section introduces a somewhat formal order based on readings in the *Lutheran Book of Worship*, providing readings and devotional possibilities for several days in each of the four weeks of Advent. The "collects," or prayers of the gathered Christian community, help us to remember that though we may pray by ourselves, we are never alone, for we are in the company of the whole Church throughout all of time.

May your Advent path help you to experience God's time in your daily walk.

Weekly Devotional Thoughts

Week 1.

Collect from *LBW:* "Stir up your power, O Lord, and come. Protect us by your strength and save us from the threatening dangers of our sins, for you live and reign with the Father and the Holy Spirit, one God, now and forever. Amen."

MATTHEW 24: 37-44

"YOU DO NOT KNOW WHAT HOUR YOUR LORD IS COMING...."

This Sunday we lit the first candle on the big Advent wreath in the Chapel, and the sense of countdown has begun. My date book is beginning to fill up in a frightening way. My life seems to be filled completely with appointments, deadlines, schedules for everything. But in this reading, when Jesus talks about His appearance at the end of time, He says it will be a surprise. That makes an odd contrast, actually, with the way we count down each day till Christmas, or the end of the semester. I get very confused when I try to think about which way to live; do I prepare for surprise, or get better at time management? As always, I need your help, Lord, for the simplest decisions.

ISAIAH 64: 1-8

"WE ARE THE WORK OF YOUR HAND...."

What a powerful reading! Mountains shaking, heavens tearing apart, nations trembling! Isaiah gives a dramatic turn to my thoughts about this time of the year. The first time, Jesus came in a very quiet way, but this last coming will let everybody know what's happening. Most of the time I don't think about those "end times," but when I do, I really like thinking about everybody finally knowing that God is God. It's like, Yes! We were right to be on His side all this time. No more of those arguments about whether God exists. When I think about it that way, I'm completely with Isaiah— "Oh, that you would tear apart the heavens and come down," NOW!

PSALM 25:1-9
"SHOW ME YOUR WAYS, O LORD; TEACH ME YOUR PATHS...."
Today I'm back down to earth. Till the end times, it's just one day after another here and back to the hard work of learning to live according to God's plan. You have the plan, Lord, and I need to learn it, which means patience, and then more patience. Show me, teach me, lead me. And I suppose that means not standing around waiting for those mountains to shake, but just doing my work for class, helping a neighbor do her grocery shopping, getting these assignments done on time. It's not dramatic, but, as this reading says, "...the humble he teaches his way." And that's me.

Week 2.

Collect from *LBW:* "Stir up our hearts, O Lord, to prepare the way for your only Son. By His coming give us strength in our conflicts and shed light on our path through the darkness of this world; through your Son, Jesus Christ our Lord, who lives and reigns with you and the Holy Spirit, one God, now and forever. Amen."

ROMANS 15: 4-13
"RECEIVE ONE ANOTHER, JUST AS CHRIST RECEIVED US...."
Oh, there's patience again, and you know, Lord, this place needs patience. Just when everything seems to be sweetness and light, I have to deal with these supposed "fellow Christians" I live with. How can a person be "like-minded" with people who are just wrong?! I don't see how we can sort out these disagreements just because we all happen to believe in Jesus as our Savior. Help me to take this reading seriously; we're all in need of help, and that bond is greater than any division. It doesn't feel that way, but I want to believe it. Give me strength—and patience, of course.

MARK 1: 1-8
"ONE COMES AFTER ME WHO IS MIGHTIER THAN I...."
John the Baptist—now there's a character! I know that if he were here, some security person would throw him out. He sounds like a total nutcase, and also like the people I walk way around on the sidewalk when I'm in the city and some strange, dirty person is preaching in that weird way. But John was right—this was the Savior that God promised. If I learn from John's example, and believe that he was telling the truth, what about those street preachers that make me very nervous? Are they your messengers, too?

More about messengers in this reading. The clue seems to be that if they are your messengers, they really do "prepare the way." They are not about themselves and their projects, but keeping pointing away from themselves and toward you. They are the helpers to those who are seeking you. So, in some sense, I can't tell who is a messenger unless I am seeking you myself, and that will help me to decide. People who heard John the Baptist, if they were truly looking for you, were helped to find you by his message. That's what I need to keep central in my thinking. Lord, I trust you will keep calling me in the direction that leads to you, and all you would have me do.

Week 3.

Collect from *LBW*: "Almighty God, you once called John the Baptist to give witness to the coming of your son and to prepare His way. Grant us, your people, the wisdom to see your purpose today and the openness to hear your will, that we may witness to Christ's coming and so prepare His way; through your Son, Jesus Christ our Lord, who lives and reigns with you and the Holy Spirit, one God, now and forever. Amen."

MATTHEW 11:2-11
"...OR DO WE LOOK FOR ANOTHER?"

"Looking" must be the key word for this season. I spent two hours yesterday looking for references for an assignment, and then went shopping with my friends, endlessly looking for the right present for my mom. And, in the religious sense, I'm supposed to be looking for the coming of Jesus. But this always feels odd; I don't have to do any looking because I already know Jesus, I already believe. Looking for "another" seems beside the point somehow. I wouldn't think of looking for another, would I? But the things that convince me of Jesus being the right one are not the things mentioned here; in my world, the blind are still blind, the dead are still dead. Help me to understand why these painful truths are true in my world, even though Jesus is the one you sent.

ISAIAH 61: 1-3, 10-11.
"TO PROCLAIM LIBERTY TO THE CAPTIVES...."

What a scary world that would be, with all the criminals running around loose! It seems to me that the perfect world that Isaiah describes would be just fine without this feature. Probably he means that people who are captive to their addictions or to their natural bad instincts would be freed from them. It's odd though that Jesus' life on earth, if it was like this prophecy from Isaiah, was characterized by actually making blind people see and raising up people from death, but not getting anybody out of jail. If Jesus was saying that being blind was not your fault, is that true of being captive also? That doesn't sound like the criminal justice system I recognize or want. Who are the captives these verses are talking about? Am I, too, a captive? Come into my prison, Lord, and free me by your power. Break the shackles of my mind and heart, and liberate me for true servanthood.

LUKE 3: 7-18.
"TEACHER, WHAT SHALL WE DO?'

This reading seems to have more bad news than good news, even though it is supposed to be the gospel. John has instructions for everybody, and they seem pretty harsh. It sounds like I can only escape that "unquenchable fire" by giving away half of what I have. A dollar or two for the Salvation Army probably won't suffice. Maybe none of it matters anyway, for "already now the ax is laid to the root of the tree," John says. It's too late to change my ways. Except, of course, that when the ax had done its work, it brought down Jesus, the one whose coming John announced. Or perhaps that ax got used instead to nail Jesus to the dry lumber made from that tree. Prune away the dead branches of my heart, O Lord, and burn clean a place that you might live within me.

Week 4.

Collect from *LBW:* "Stir up your power, O Lord, and come. Take away the hindrance of our sins and make us ready for the celebration of your birth, that we may receive you in joy and serve you always; for you live and reign with the Father and the Holy Spirit, one God, now and forever. In Christ's name we pray. Amen."

PSALM 24.
"WHO IS THIS KING OF GLORY?"

A question and answer session, and for us today. The answer seems easy—the King of glory is the Lord strong and mighty, etc. I don't have to be part of a *Messiah* sing-along to get that one right. But what do these antique terms mean for life at this moment? Jesus was not mighty in battle. But He is the one we're talking about these days, His coming, His great arrival. Christianity says that this great King arrives, not though actual gates into a literal city, but into hearts—into my heart, into my spirit, my inner life, my deepest self. Help me to get a welcome mat out, Lord, to welcome your Word into my self once again.

LUKE 1:26-38.
"LET IT BE TO ME ACCORDING TO YOUR WILL."

Mary's example is wonderful and I could spend much more time on it than I do, even though during Morning Prayer at the Chapel we sing her song every day while we pray the O Antiphons..." My soul magnifies the Lord, and my spirit rejoices in God my Savior...." I hear the *Magnificat* often, but my own spirit tends to do more resisting than accepting. Those words, "let it be to me according to your will" are some of the hardest of all words for me to mean, even if I can say them easily. I really want my will to be done. Thank you, Lord, for the example of Mary, and give me some of her strength of faith in accepting your will.

"...THOUGH YOU ARE LITTLE AMONG THE THOUSANDS...."

Bigness is crucial for success, or so we're told in
marketing studies. Consolidate and win. I, too, tend to
trust bigness; who is it who wants to have the biggest,
showiest present under the tree—whether I'm giving it or
getting it? But the big towns in Judea lost out to
Bethlehem, the little hick town no one would have
remembered if one of history's greatest events hadn't
happened there. You tend to like smallness, Lord, which I
forget too often. Birth is a small event too, one at a time,
a real one-on-one event, but one at a time is how you
make changes. Change me every day, a little at a time,
into the person you want me to be, and maybe I'll surprise
people, too, like Bethlehem, "little among the thousands."

Celebrating Lives of Faith

(the following usually fall during Advent)

November 30
Andrew, Apostle

Almighty God, as the apostle Andrew readily obeyed the call of Christ and followed Him without delay, grant that we, called by your holy Word, may offer ourselves in glad obedience to your service; through your Son, Jesus Christ our Lord. Amen.

December 6
Nicolas, Bishop of Myra

> O COME, LITTLE CHILDREN, OH COME, ONE AND ALL
> TO BETHLEHEM HASTE, TO THE MANGER SO SMALL
> GOD'S SON FOR A GIFT HAS BEEN SENT US THIS NIGHT
> TO BE OUR REDEEMER, OUR JOY AND DELIGHT.

Thank you, Lord God, for the life of your servant Nicolas. Though much about him is hidden, his story encourages us to love, protect, and cherish children. May I be bold in facing those who in carelessness, greed, or viciousness bring children's lives into harm, and give us grace to remember, as Nicolas did, that what I give to children, I give to you. In the name of the blessed Christ Child. Amen.

December 14
John of the Cross (1591) and
Teresa of Avila (1582)

> LET NOTHING DISTURB YOU
> NOTHING FRIGHTEN YOU,
> ALL THINGS ARE PASSING;
> PATIENT ENDURANCE
> ATTAINS ALL THINGS.
> ONE WHOM GOD POSSESSES
> LACKS NOTHING,
> FOR GOD ALONE SUFFICES.

St. Teresa of Avila

December 21
Thomas, Apostle

Lord God, we give thanks for our brother Thomas. When he doubted, he did not turn away privately into his own fears, but rather, seeking out the presence of fellow disciples, he came closer to you. Help me to turn my face toward you, to ask and even to demand that your certainty reach out to gather me closer. Help me to echo the Believing Thomas in his affirmation: "My Lord and my God!" Amen.

Prayers of the Season

Homesickness

I don't know whether I can stand it much longer—I miss my home so much! If people are supposed to grow up and find their own place in the world, why is it so hard for me to be away from my family? I thought by now that my life here at the University would take away completely that horrible, empty feeling I had when I first came. But it still comes back; some stupid TV ad can make me cry, and I don't want to feel like that! Help me to know where my true place is, and to trust that you, Lord, will be with me there. Amen.

New friends

It hit me today while I was thinking about my shopping list for Christmas—I have tons of new friends! What a great thing that is, except for my budget. Each of these new people in my life is valuable and special. They are talented and funny and smart, and I hope they will be my friends forever. Bless every one of them, Lord, keep them safe while we're apart over break—and make them still like me, even if I can only afford to give them cards for Christmas! In the name of Christ, my truest friend. Amen.

Advent-Christmas Vespers

Tonight is the Advent-Christmas Vespers, and I want to feel the excitement that people say is part of it. Help me to be open-hearted, to let go of my efforts to be cool and sophisticated. Thank you, Lord, for the hard work that many people have done to get ready for this—from moving the pews and decorating the Chapel to practicing instruments and rehearsing the readings. Give me just a few moments where I forget myself in the joy of recognizing the meaning of this holy season. Amen.

Renewed energy

Am I the only one who feels like my batteries are shutting down during these darker days? As the winter comes on, I really get down—and then even downer. We haven't seen the sun for days, and I feel like a candle with a snuffer just over it. Everybody else is running around like crazy, but I want to hiberate. Give me strength to recognize this feeling and then get on with it, Lord. Amen.

Focus

This is such a busy time of the semester that I hardly stop for breath; sometimes it's hard to remember that learning is the reason I'm here. There are many things I want to do to make the season special that I tend to miss the point that you, Lord, have made it special already. Remind me to take quiet time for prayer and praise, and to slow down the pace of my frantic busyness. One of my profs said today that we're not thinking enough; "You spend enough time," she said, "but what kind of time is it?" One of many things I need your help with, Lord. In Christ's name. Amen.

Facing exams

Here we are at the crunch time, and I'm feeling pretty good. In a way, I'm really curious to see what my profs are going to throw at me, because I am ready to show off what I can do. This semester I tried some new ways of studying, and they have worked well. I guess like an athlete, I am pumped and ready! Of course I have to hide this feeling from everybody but you, Lord, or I'd look like a jerk. Help me to be sensible about things like sleep and food, and to resist temptations that would mess me up. I want to do my best, and I think this time I'm ready to do it. Be with me. Amen.

Struggling with exams

This is the most terrible time of the year. How can I be glad and happy about Christmas when I'm scared to death? I knew this semester was going to be a bear, and that's how it's turning out. I'm working, but nothing registers—my brain is not making the connections it should, and I feel like everything in it has been in a blender. What is going to happen? My fear gets going, and then that's really it—I can't think at all. Please give me some guidance and support, Lord. Some of this may be my fault, and I'll try to do better next semester, but I need to know that you care about me, however my GPA turns out. Amen.

From the Chapel

Voices in the Wilderness

Isaiah 40:3-5
Isaiah 55:10-13

"In Advent we hear voices crying in the wilderness. The wilderness isn't supposed to have voices. That's what makes it 'wilderness.' Howling jackals, or the incessant moaning of the wind? Yes. But not voices.

"Our English word wilderness means 'place of wild things.' The Bible's Greek word means 'place of abandonment.' The still more ancient Hebrew word means literally 'somewhere beyond words.'

"Most of us know that place beyond words, and the farther in we go, the greater our distance from home. Words like layoff, inoperable, terminal, divorce, or suicide often banish us to the place that words can't describe.

"Then we walk a road we can't name, in a place beyond description, without a word of explanation.

"Our faith, and the story it clings to, provides words for our frequent, continual treks through the wilderness. One word tells us we're never alone. 'My God, my God, why...?' Yes, even He stumbled into the wordless abyss.

"Ultimately, there is no answer, no reason why.

"There is only that word calling from somewhere up ahead (or is it from behind?): 'Come hooooooome! You are mine, dear child! Your place is here!'

"The road home is on most maps. The blue highways, the red ones, even the gray, dotted lines between the tiny burgs—they're all roads home just as surely as they lead farther and deeper into the wilderness. All depends on the voice that calls you, the hand of the creator that will never let go of you no matter how lost you get.

"The road home leads up the aisle to the altar where we stop for a meal. And it leads straight back out again to the places where we hurl words into the wordlessness: 'Come home! You belong to us!'

"O God, whose word once broke into the formless void and made this world and all of us in it, speak now your Word into the silence and emptiness of our lives. Call us, gather us, and make us your own for all eternity. Amen."

Frederick Niedner

Words and Stones in the Dust

"When they kept on questioning him, Jesus straightened up and said to them, 'Let anyone among you who is without sin be the first to throw a stone at her.' And once again He bent down and wrote on the ground.

"We cannot read this gospel lesson without questions. One, for instance, is that the law being quoted from Leviticus 20:10 says, 'both the adulterer and the adulteress shall be put to death.' I have always wondered where the man is in this story. But there is no answer to that question.

"Another mystery is the writing. Of all the relics of Jesus' life that might have been saved, surely the most precious to the community of believers in the Word would have been these unknown words—but they were written in the dust. What a loss, not only to the Church's history of relicolatry, but also to theology, to the whole huge company of readers and writers about the Word.

"What if you could have, for your own written words, the ultimate primary source material! How much we would love to have them—but they were written in the dust. They might have answered innumerable puzzles, or stood as the immutable testament to Jesus' view of Himself and His mission. But they were written in the dust, and like the dust, they were blown away across the dusty square in front of the temple, and our questions about the only writing we know Jesus ever did will not be answered either.

"And then, lastly, there are those unused stones. They lie there on the ground, where they have been dropped, and the dust blows around them while Jesus and the woman hold their short solitary dialogue. The stones were brought by people who were experts with stones. You can bet that they knew all the variations, the niceties, the ins and outs of the stone-throwing business. For there are 17 separate offenses in Leviticus 20, each with separate degrees of punishment, from being 'cast out,' to being 'burned in the fire,' to being 'stoned with stones.' Yes, this was a group that had studied the stone-throwing side of godliness; they were keen, they were knowledgeable, they were zealous. Now, they thought, they had the perfect opportunity to make their stones do double duty, to kill, in fact, the proverbial two birds with one stone. Make Jesus disagree with Moses, show Jesus soft on stoning, and not only do you get the adulteress, you knock Jesus too.

"Jesus' answer catches them, though. With a meekness wiser than serpents, he proposes that they consider another dimension of Moses' law. Put like that—to be able to throw a stone, you must be someone who could not possibly be a target—nobody could be a stone-thrower. The silence falls, the stones clunk into the dust, and Jesus keeps looking down at His writing. Finally, the silence is so great that He looks up. Only the woman, and the silently blowing dust are there.

"'Has no one condemned you?'

"'No one, Lord.'

"'Neither do I condemn you; go, and do not sin again.'

"Now where are we in this picture? I think we have to revise it somewhat for today, because for us, the processes of religious law have become internalized to a great extent. No church committees come out to stone the sinners these days. I doubt that one of us will ever face a board of elders armed with stones. Yet the condemnations of the law have not ceased to operate. It is mostly that today we, as righteous law dealers, throw the stones at ourselves as helpless sinners. We may not often recognize that our self-hate and our inward bitterness are the stones of our own throwing, but I think it is often so. Huddled against the Temple wall, part of me cringes helplessly while the other part, a zealous gleam in the eye, throws the accusations—'You loveless hypocrite! You ungrateful daughter! You selfish, lazy mother'"

"Or, fill them in for yourself: 'You wimp! You mess-up, You alcoholic creep, you no-good, time-wasting failure!' To that part of me that is accused, Jesus says, 'I do not condemn you.' And the stones drop to the ground. Because this is what it means when we say, 'Jesus has taken my sins away'—it means that the stones are now for Him. He has the authority to say where the stones should be thrown, and He says they should not be thrown at us, but at Him.

"And so I wonder what He wrote as He knelt there and listened to His stones drop into the dust and silence by the temple, knowing that they were now His stones. Remember that next time you get ready to throw one."

Gail McGrew Eifrig
A homily from the years she served on the Morning Prayer staff

The Day of the Lord

Amos 5:18-24
Romans 13:8-14

"In our lessons for this day, Amos and Paul are speaking to the expectations of God's people.

"Amos' people expect the Day of the Lord to be a day when the Lord rewards them for their solemn assemblies and sacrifices. The People of Israel judge their worship worthy of a blessing, but Amos knows they like nothing better in their solemn assemblies than the sound of their own voices, and in the midst of their sacrifices they're already licking their lips for the roast beef.

"So Amos tells his people their Day of the Lord will be darkness and not light, a fast and not a feast, judgment and not blessing, for God is not amused. He takes no delight in their solemn assemblies and He despises their sacrifices.

"Amos does not go on to say the People of Israel should enter more heartily into their worship. Amos is no cheerleader. Someone else can shout, 'Bring on more bulls!' Nor does he urge them to feel their worship more deeply. Amos is no therapist. Someone else can lead the primal screams. No, for Amos, true worship begins deeper than enthusiasm and sincerity.

True worship, true lives

"True worship begins in true lives. What was lacking in Israel's ceremonies and sacrifices was not enthusiasm or sincerity, but truth. And so Amos arouses Israel to be up and about seeking justice and righteousness among the people. Perhaps then they will find true lives to join to their lips in serving the Lord.

"Otherwise, says Amos, the Day of the Lord for the People of Israel will be a great irony. They will get the opposite off what they expect. Just as one thinks he has escaped a lion, he runs into a bear. Just as he thinks he is home free and leaning on his wall, a snake will strike. Updated, that irony is like a professor who receives a raise in his wages only to discover the cost of living has gone up twice as much, or like a college student who finally achieves his degree only to discover that jobs in his field are not to be had.

"Paul also speaks to the expectations of the people of God in his day. The Christians at Rome are expecting the Day of the Lord to be a day of judgment. Indeed, some Christians are so eager for the Lord's Day that they are already doing His work of judgment for Him. In Paul's letter to the Romans we see Christians judging one another more or less Christian by what they eat and drink, or do not eat and drink, or what days they keep as holy days. This judging, they think, is doing the Lord's work until He comes. This judging, they sincerely believe, is what is expected of them while they are expecting Him.

"Paul is appalled, and he appeals to them to wake up, get their Christian clothes on, for the Day of the Lord is at hand. This means loving their brothers by being far less careful to judge them and far more caring to build them up. Let each brother honor Christ in his own way, for the Day of the Lord does not mean food and drink, who eats and who fasts, but 'righteousness in the Holy Spirit.'

True and false expectations
"Both Amos and Paul correct the expectations of the people of God about the day of the Lord, both their expectations of God and their expectations of themselves. The people of God are always tempted to confuse judgment and justice, making judgment their work and justice God's work. They judge themselves worthy and right and ask God to seek justice in the world and edify their neighbors. Thus, prophets and apostles find full-time jobs reminding God's people that judgment is God's work in his own good time and justice is their work all the time.

'Let justice roll down like waters and righteousness like an ever-flowing stream.'

"Certainly that is a prophetic and apostolic word the people of God also need to hear today. And perhaps another word, too. For Amos and Paul, at least the people of God had some expectations of God and themselves, as wrongheaded as those expectations were. But there is something worse than false expectations, and that is no expectations at all. False expectations can be corrected and idols can be cleansed. But where the people of God expect nothing there is the deepest sadness. It's like a University celebrating fifty years of being disturbed by Christian auspices, but its chapel, like this one today, is adorned only with pictures from its past and no picture attempts a vision for its future.

Vocation and expectation

"The world word of the Lord, therefore, is to remind the people of God that they can live expectantly on their gracious God and have some great expectations of themselves. For the people of God gathered at a University, this means being reminded to expect Christ in the general studies of the University where new dimensions of human possibility and human need are revealed, and to expect Christ in the professional studies of the University where a vocation for rising to those human possibilities and meeting those human needs may be revealed. Surely we are not solemnly assembled to pursue mere careers.

"For today is not only the first day of the rest of our lives. Today is also a Day of the Lord, and tomorrow is a Day of the Lord, and so on day by day—until the last Day of the Lord when we rest from our lives in Him who is no surprise."

Richard Lee

Of the Same Mind

"If there is any encouragement in Christ, any consolation
from love, any sharing in the Spirit, any compassion and
sympathy, make my joy complete: be of the same mind,
having the same love, being in full accord and of one mind.
Do nothing from selfish ambition or conceit, but in humility
regard others as better than yourselves. Let each of you look
not to your own interests, but to the interests of others. Let
the same mind be in you that was in Christ Jesus,

> *who, though he was in the form of God,*
> *did not regard equality with God*
> *as something to be exploited,*
> *but emptied himself*
> *taking the form of a slave,*
> *being born in human likeness.*

Philippians 2:1-7

"When we look around us here in this community we may
note many differences, differences that can put stresses
and strains on unity, but perhaps by God's grace we can
also look around and see the marks of a community
shaped by the presence of Christ, a people among whom
there is encouragement in Christ when people grow
weary, consolation when people are hurting, the kind of
sharing in the Spirit that builds people up, and
compassion and sympathy whenever anyone has need.
And perhaps with the Philippian community, we can start
there to begin to live the unity that is God's gift to us also.

"At first glance—or even at second glance—it might seem
that Paul is asking the Philippians—and us—to do the
impossible. Or if it's not impossible, at the very least, it
seems to be unhealthy. Is he asking us to all think alike—
to have the same mind? Is he asking us to become
doormats for other people to walk on? I think not.

"Rather, the oneness of mind is to be found in the mind of
Christ. And here Paul quotes a beautiful hymn—perhaps a
favorite piece of the liturgy that he and the Philippians

sang together—a hymn that describes so beautifully Jesus Christ's self-emptying servanthood that led all the way to the cross. There is no self-deprecating, false modesty here, only fulfillment of the true vocation of Jesus, the Christ. And what seems to be the end is really the beginning of Jesus' exaltation by God, an exaltation that ends with everyone in all creation worshiping Jesus Christ as Lord. You can almost hear the hymn—the organ with all the stops open and brass and tympani and the huge congregation singing with one voice.

"But that promise is not yet quite fulfilled for the Philippians or for us. We are still here in this fragile community trying with fear and trembling to live the unity that is God's gift.

"Perhaps you have known a relationship where you were so tuned in to each other that you almost knew what the other one was thinking and sometimes you even found yourselves thinking the same things at the same time. Perhaps you have known such a relationship. Paul encourages the Philippians and us in such a relationship with Christ Jesus.

"We who are in Christ Jesus have access to the mind of Christ. As we attune ourselves to that one through hearing the word, using the sacraments, praying, being part of the give and take of the community of faith, talking with each other, more and more the mind of Christ becomes our mind and we can see those other people—even with all our differences—not as threats or competitors, but as people in whom God is also working, as people who like us are trying to become attuned to the mind of Christ— people whom we can love, at least once in a while, with Christ's own self-giving love. Nothing could make God—or us—happier. May it be so. Amen."

Louise Williams,
excerpted from The Cresset, 1997, pp. 10-11

Come
and
Worship
Him

Designer Unknown, December 1965

Christmas

The Season of Christmas

Most of the world that celebrates Christmas does so amidst the bustle of a million distractions. Shopping, travel, and other preparations can overwhelm us to the point that we nearly forget the birth we mean to commemorate with all our efforts.

This should not surprise us. After all, the birth of the Messiah came at a time equivalent to what would happen if we combined April 15th, tax day, with the day of a general election. Quite predictably, there was no room in the inn—not to mention the board rooms, government halls, shopping malls, and ballrooms—for Mary to birth her child.

So, Jesus' mom laid her baby in the only quiet place she and Joseph could find, the ancient equivalent of a gas station garage, next to an old motel, amidst the tools, batteries, and discarded tires.

Ironically, Valparaiso's busy campus becomes one of those quiet places at Christmas. The parking lots are empty and the campus rests quietly. Even the international students, who remain in the residence halls through other breaks and vacations mostly find places to go for this season.

Sunday worship continues at 10:30 a.m. in Gloria Christi Chapel. On Christmas Eve at 11:00 p.m., Gloria Christi fills for a candlelight Eucharist graced by a choir of faculty, staff, and a few young people home for the holidays from other colleges and universities. When the faithful few sing, "Silent Night, Holy Night," that song rings true in every way.

And there, as in every other place where Christians find a quiet moment amidst the season's inescapable commotion, the Christ child is born once more.

Celebrating Lives of Faith

December 26
St. Stephen, Deacon and Martyr

Lord, those who tend the garments, cook the meals, and watch out for the children and the elderly do your work just as surely as those who go to the big meetings, preach eloquent sermons, and stone dangerous heretics. Help us like your servant Stephen to find joy in serving you quietly. Let us speak your truth with courage when the time for that comes. Then help us even with our dying breaths to love all your children, including those who prove to be our enemies. In the name of Jesus. Amen.

December 27
St. John, Apostle and Evangelist

FOR ALL YOUR SAINTS IN WARFARE,
FOR ALL YOUR SAINTS AT REST,
YOUR HOLY NAME, O JESUS,
FOREVER MORE BE BLEST
FOR YOU HAVE WON THE BATTLE
THAT THEY MIGHT WEAR THE CROWN;
AND NOW THEY SHINE IN GLORY
REFLECTED FROM YOUR THRONE.

FOR YOUR BELOVED DISCIPLE
EXILED TO PATMOS' SHORE,
AND FOR HIS FAITHFUL RECORD,
WE PRAISE YOU EVERMORE.
PRAISE FOR THE MYSTIC VISION
HIS WORDS TO US UNFOLD.
INSTILL IN US HIS LONGING
YOUR GLORY TO BEHOLD.

(LBW #177: 1, 8)

Special Days

December 24

Christmas Eve

Opening collect from *LBW:* "Almighty God, you made this holy night shine with the brightness of the true Light. Grant that here on earth we may walk in the light of Jesus' presence and in the last day wake to the brightness of his glory; through your Son, Jesus Christ our Lord, who lives and reigns with you and the Holy Spirit, one God, now and forever. Amen."

reading: John 1:1-14. "...and the light shines in darkness, and the darkness has not overcome it."

Meditation

This quiet moment brings me all alone, silent and awestruck, to the stable in the dark of night. Who can understand this wonderful thing, the subject of so much praise and joy? There seems to be no way to take it in, and yet the very awesomeness of it can be overwhelmed by all kinds of wordy, worldly noise. In this beautiful night, pain and suffering seems far away, and yet it has its place, even here. For this is not any baby, but the one who will suffer everything that human life can endure, and worse.

The parts of the story are simple and familiar. How could we do without one piece of the story—the angels, the manger, the young mother, the worried guardian, the shepherds. I know it well, and yet its meaning is bigger than I can ever manage. Here, after ages of saying this over and over to people, using tablets of the Law, and covenants, and marches out of Egypt, and all kinds of other messages and techniques, God uses this baby for His best offer: "Come closer; let us be as close as mother and baby. I am the God who has always loved you; now, see if you can't love me back." And, with all its world-shaking significance, it is for me, to make a difference in my life. Just for a moment, let me be still enough to feel the wonder.

A Stable Lamp is Lighted

A STABLE LAMP IS LIGHTED
WHOSE GLOW SHALL WAKE THE SKY,
THE STARS SHALL BEND THEIR VOICES
AND EVERY STONE SHALL CRY.
AND EVERY STONE SHALL CRY, AND STRAW LIKE GOLD
SHALL SHINE
A BARN SHALL HARBOR HEAVEN,
A STALL BECOME A SHRINE.

(LBW #74)

Closing Prayer

Lord God, come into my waiting heart and life. Light up with your radiance the dark corners of my fearful self, and make me acknowledge myself as the beloved receiver of this wonderful gift. In His very name I pray. Amen.

Prayers of the Season

Contemplating abundance

Lord, I have so much—and so does almost everyone I know. Here in the Christmas season it's hard to escape the idea that there is just an endless supply of things. Keep me aware of the value—and the limitations—of things. Let me keep in my heart somewhere the capacity of a little child to marvel not only at inventions and gadgets, but also at simple things like boxes and packing bubbles. Let my pleasure in things spill over into generosity, so that sharing things is as good as having them. Amen.

Giving and receiving gifts

Why is there that moment of awkwardness, God, when all the shopping and selecting and buying and wrapping is over—in that moment of giving or receiving a gift? Is there perhaps an intimacy in that exchange, which we gloss over through ritual but can never completely erase? Or might it be in that moment of giving that through the cracks of our universe I am in touch with you, the Giver, and in that moment of receiving know your yearning heart opens to all we can offer you? Amen.

Christ's Birth

Gracious God, the Holy Scriptures tell of Your son becoming one of us. His beginning was much like ours, a person dependent on the love and care of others. Like us, His birth evoked moments of unexpected adoration and alarming acts of insecurity. In today's world of slick and distorted Christmas advertising, keep us clearheaded and open-hearted to the real meaning of Jesus' birth. While there is plenty to distract us during these holidays, and there is much that would undermine our faith in you, grant us the capacity to accept Christ's birth as a divine mystery that reflects Your enduring and sacrificial love for us. In the name of Jesus we pray. Amen.

New Year

"Eternal God, You know well enough how I treated this past year. Forgive me for squandering, misappropriating, and just plain frittering away so much time. The good news is that with You there is always a new day. Even a new year! Thank you for the opportunities before me this year. Opportunities to explore promising ideas, serve those in need, deepen treasured relationships, refine my abilities, correct past mistakes, and celebrate Your enduring grace and mercy. Every day is Your gift, Lord. Keep me grateful. I pray in Christ's name. Amen."

William O. Karpenko II

Winter weather

The winter is here for certain now, Lord, and I love this clear, cold season. All the foggy uncertainty of fall is blown away, and the earth is as chilly and plain and honest as it's going to get. Let me enjoy the sense of your power in the wind, and your own eye for beauty in the sweep of snow across the landscape. Keep me safe from winter's dangers, even as I enjoy its strong grace. Amen.

From the Chapel

At one of Valpo's Christmas Eve services a few years ago, the Rev. David Kehret, associate dean of the Chapel and associate pastor to the University since 1984, continued his "Chronicles of Vera Cruz University" with this story.

Jimmy's Christmas

"Life has been a grim affair for Jimmy. In his four short years and running he has seen more grief than most folks will experience in their entire lives. Jimmy lives with his mother, Debbie, and his sister, Diane, who is old enough to go to school now, in a new place where they moved at the end of summer. Jimmy took the move right in stride since they have moved an awful lot. Here, Mom says, they can get a new start; they will have a chance for a better life. And here, Mom says, Dad won't be nearby, which is a comfort for Jimmy, because his experiences of Dad, though few, have been experiences of terror which Jimmy is already pushing back into the shadows of his young mind.

"Though Mom says there are already a lot of good things happening to them in this new place, Christmas this year is going to be meager. Still, Mom did get out the box of Christmas things which has always moved with them, and she took out a green and silver garland which she taped to the wall in the shape of a Christmas tree. There are six, shiny, Christmas balls hanging on it, and there is one string of tiny colored lights that Mom plugged in below the tree.

"Mom also took the empty Christmas box, put it upside down under the tree, and covered it with a green cloth. Then from another box packed inside the Christmas box she took out the nativity scene, ceramic pieces which she set up on the green cloth—a stable, Mary and Joseph, a manger, shepherds and sheep, wise men and camels, and even an angel. But when you move a lot things get broken, so the angel had only one wing until Mom attached the other wing with some tape. It wiggles, but that's OK when the angel flies. And one of the camels has only three legs,

66

but if you lean it against one of the wise men it won't fall over, and you can't even tell one leg is missing. And the baby that goes in the manger, the baby Jesus, for as long as Jimmy can remember its plaster face has been chipped.

"Jimmy spent hours this past week sitting at the nativity scene there at the foot of his Christmas tree on the wall. He makes the angel fly down from heaven. He rearranges the sheep and the shepherds. He moves the wise men and camels around, always making certain the three-legged camel can still stand. He reaches into the manger and takes out the baby Jesus, the Jesus without a face, and holds it close to himself, loving it. Then he kisses it and puts it back in the manger again.

"It might have been just a matter of chance, if there be such a thing in our universe, that Sara and Pamela and their sorority sisters from the campus of Vera Cruz University got the names this year of Debbie and Diane and Jimmy in the annual adopt-a-family gift program. The entire sorority has been on a shopping spree you wouldn't believe these past days, and they have purchased bright Christmas paper and have wrapped each gift with care, with ribbons and bows. Then yesterday afternoon, late, as the orange, winter sun was hanging just over the horizon and everything was finally in order, Sara and Pamela and Angie—three young women bearing gifts—went trooping off into the neighborhood near campus. They carefully matched street signs and house numbers against a scrap of paper they held, until nervously they filed up a walk and onto the small porch of the apartment they were looking for and rang the doorbell.

"Debbie, who is barely older than the three young women at her door, was overwhelmed, and she cried. She managed to ask them to step inside, which they did, then she cried again as one whole stack of gifts was put into her hands. Yet another stack of presents was put into the arms of little Diane, leaving only Pamela to kneel down in front of Jimmy with her arms still full. 'Jimmy, these are for you.'

"Jimmy just stood there, his eyes growing bigger and bigger with excitement, while Mom whispered, 'Jimmy, what do you say?'

"Jimmy knew how to say 'Thank you,' but those words just didn't seem to measure up to the monumental event that was happening to him. Pamela tried to put the presents into his hands. The stack was half as tall as Jimmy, so together they set the gifts down against the wall under the Christmas tree beside the nativity scene.

"Suddenly Jimmy reached into the nativity scene and snatched up the tiny Jesus without a face. He clung to it while he looked into Pamela's eyes which were now like swimming pools. Then he threw his arms around Pamela and kissed her and absolutely broke her heart.

"It is still ten days until Christmas, and Mom has said no gifts will be unwrapped until Christmas Eve. Until then they can look at them, which all three of them have been doing, and they can touch them if they are careful. You can believe Jimmy will be spending hours over these next days there at the foot of his tree, next to the nativity scene and the presents. He will rearrange the shepherds and the wise men, and he will hold the baby Jesus lovingly. But he will also reach over to pick up this present or that and shake it gently, wondering what might be inside.

"When Christmas comes Jimmy will discover a blue and red, warm, woolen hat, and warm mittens to match, and a Garfield sweatshirt with sweatpants to go with it. There will be a big, picture book about the first Christmas, and a teddy bear to cuddle and a box of Lego's to learn to build things with. And Jimmy's heart will be filled with an inexpressible joy, a joy nearly as great as that which has already come into his dark, December days. For in these winter days, for the first time in Jimmy's life, Jimmy's Jesus has a face."

David H. Kehret

*Over a generation before Jimmy's Christmas, V.U. President
O. P. Kretzmann many times inspired the Valparaiso
University community's Christmas celebrations. In this
piece from 1950, Dr. Kretzmann pointed the way to
Bethlehem's stable.*

Following the Shepherds

"To reach Bethlehem, one must follow the shepherds. No
questioning on their part when they heard the angel's
message and the angelic chorus. No huddle and hesitation,
no concern about the sheep, no fear of the night. But hear
them saying in concert: 'Let us be off to Bethlehem and see
this thing that the Lord made known to us.' For them
Bethlehem was near and the road smooth, in spite of the
darkness of the night, in spite of fences and hedges, in spite
of scanty clues. Or follow the Magi. They saw the star in the
East, and they followed the star. They, too, asked no
questions. They did no checking and cross-checking in the
ancient sacred books. No loitering on the way. But they
started out resolutely, took the shortest route to Bethlehem,
and found the Child.

"Oh, to find Bethlehem! Once more to kneel before that
Child with penitent heart and to confess: 'Thou hast
redeemed me, a lost and condemned sinner, purchased and
won me from all sins, from death and from the power of the
devil.' Once more to know that this Child is above all. To
know that even in His lowly poverty He towers as a mighty
Everest above all humans, above all angels, above cherubim
and seraphim. To know once again that this Child belongs to
that glorious, holy Trinity of Father, Son, and Holy Ghost, of
one substance and of majesty co-equal. Once more to see in
this Child not only the Babe of Bethlehem, but also the Lamb
of Calvary, the High Priest in the heavenly sanctuary, and
the returning Lion of Judah. Oh, to know in these trying
days that this Child is above all, the Lord of men and angels,
the Lord of all worlds, the Lord of time and space, the Lord
of heaven and eternity, the Lord of all."

O.P. Kretzmann, Christmas Garlands
(Chicago: Walther League, 1950), p. 83.

Who Pays?

(A homily for the Feast of the Holy Innocents, Martyrs, December 28)

Jeremiah 31:15-17
Matthew 2:13-18

"Children most always pay more dearly than parents for the parents' sins. Egypt's firstborn died because of Pharaoh's stubborn heart. David's son paid the ultimate price for the lustful eye that brought Uriah's wife to the palace bedroom. Psalm 137 asks God to smash the heads of babies for their parents' lack of compassion.

"King Herod listened to the Magi's tale and then slaughtered all male infants of Bethlehem. He'd likely never remember giving the order. He'd already killed 70 of his own sons lest they grow up to challenge him.

"Of all the innocents slain in humanity's endless war on itself, we remember Herod's victims because Matthew saw in their tragic end a link to Israel's long journey out of slavery. Once again a wicked king destroys infants. A man named Joseph dreams dreams and travels to Egypt. Once more a single infant escapes the carnage to become a savior.

"This time the story runs backwards, however, as the prophet Hosea had threatened, and the surviving child would work toward the redemption of every people, including Egypt and Edom.

"We remember today every kind of slaughtered innocent caught in the world's crossfire, those killed by warlords, crusaders, Nazis, drunk drivers, stray bullets, or immature parents.

"God does not forget these lives, brief as they were, nor is their lifeblood lost to God. With inconsolable mother Rachel, who weeps for her children because they are no more, God also weeps.

"And God promises, 'There is hope for your future; your children shall come back to their own country.'

"The child who escaped Herod will return and give his own blood that God might have forever the life of every child slaughtered in humanity's madness.

"If the child you once were died amidst one of those wicked scenes, God knows. God holds you, too, in the same embrace.

> "CHILDREN OF THE HEAV'NLY FATHER
> SAFELY IN HIS BOSOM GATHER,
> NESTLING BIRD OR STAR IN HEAVEN
> SUCH A REFUGE NE'ER WAS GIVEN.
>
> "NEITHER LIFE NOR DEATH SHALL EVER
> FROM THE LORD HIS CHILDREN SEVER,
> UNTO THEM HIS GRACE HE SHOWETH,
> AND THEIR SORROWS ALL HE KNOWETH."

(LBW #25:4)
Frederick Niedner

W.C. Brusick, February 1975

Epiphany

The Season of Epiphany

Chances are that you'll get back to this Prayer Book after all the commotions of celebrating Christmas are over. The mystery and the beauty of Christmas Eve are part of the past; it seems as though all our planning and rushing culminated in one brief, 24-hour period. But the Church has another wisdom: 12 days of Christmas and several weeks of Epiphany, which is always celebrated on the 6th of January. (Though its beginning is always the same date, Epiphany's end depends on the date of Ash Wednesday, which is variable. Check your local church bulletin!) As our lives in the everyday world get, as we like to say, "back to normal," it takes Epiphany to remind us that, after Jesus' birth in that long ago time and faraway place, nothing can ever be "normal" again.

The word "epiphany" means "showing forth," and it refers to the fact that, after the mystery of Jesus' arrival at Christmas, the next stage was His public appearance to the world. Epiphany's centerpiece is the visit of the Wise Men to the infant Jesus. Its central figures ought to be familiar to us; the Wise Men were scholars, scientists, explorers, knowledge seekers. They apparently weren't content just to repeat what their own people believed. They wanted something more; after all, we don't call them just the "Smart Men." They wanted wisdom, which meant that they wanted to know the source of all truth, and then to bring to that source the offering of themselves.

On campus during this time of year, we're always occupied with all the activity of beginning a new semester. Just surviving the gray cold or the brilliant snowy days and nights can be plenty to cope with. We make our way to our first classes, and look over new syllabi and assess each other (teachers and students) as we start the new routines. By now, routines are how we have learned to move in the University environment.

Maybe that's why it's an especially good time for us to remember the Wise Men. What are we doing here? Are we looking for the source of truth? Are we ready to give that search all we've got? When we have gathered up our treasures (our grades, our resumes, our portfolios) where will we take them as an offering?

In this section, we journey with the Wise Men through the weeks of Epiphany, dedicating ourselves to our work of learning and seeking. And remembering that, with Jesus in the world, getting back to normal is not an option.

Weekly Devotional Thoughts

Week 1

First Sunday after Epiphany

MATTHEW 3:13-17.

"...HE SAW THE SPIRIT OF GOD DESCENDING ON HIM...."

Jesus' baptism is a great moment in Christian history, but I'm really too busy with other things right now to notice. At this moment, God's voice comes directly out of heaven and announces Jesus' identity, which is really impressive. But the church doesn't celebrate this event with a festival or anything. It seems to pass by with almost no notice at all. Back to the littleness of Bethlehem, the darkness of the stable, the humility of the shepherds. Help me, Lord, to notice what's important, whether anyone makes a big deal out of it or not.

ISAIAH 42:1-7.

"I HAVE PUT MY SPIRIT UPON HIM...."

When I think about Jesus appearing, I think about love, but this prophecy has God talking mainly about justice in the world. And justice is connected with not breaking down what is already weak. I have plenty to think about with getting my life organized right now-clean laundry and getting to class on time seem to be about all I can manage. If imitating Jesus means working on justice, I don't know whether I'm up for it. Couldn't I just put that off for a few years?

"YOU ARE MY SON, MY BELOVED...."

Here's another story about Jesus' baptism, this one with more people in it—all this crowd standing around while John tells them about who Jesus is, and then the voice from heaven puts a seal of approval on it: Yes, this is the one I am sending. Impressive! If I had been in that crowd, I would know exactly what to do about following Jesus. But I wasn't there, so I just have to do the best I can. Maybe if I find the crowd around Jesus today and stick with them, everything will be clear. Lord, help me to know how I am to follow you today.

Second Sunday after the Epiphany

Collect from *LW*: "Almighty and eternal God, governor of all things in heaven and on earth, mercifully hear the prayers of your people, and grant us your peace in our days; through Jesus Christ, our Lord, who lives and reigns with you and the Holy Spirit, one god, now and forever."

PSALM 40: 1-12.
"...THE LORD TAKES THOUGHT FOR ME."

What wonderful promises I can count on, just as the Psalmist does! This is a tough time of year; even when things in general are going well, just getting around in all the cold weather can be a struggle. Not to mention that everything from flu to depression is pretty powerful in the residences right now. But I know that I can count on that "steadfast love and faithfulness," whatever winter brings. Thank you, Lord, for your constant goodness to me.

I CORINTHIANS 6:12-20.
"THEREFORE GLORIFY GOD IN YOUR BODY."

This reading gets right at the heart of a real problem—what is the relation between my body and the connection I'm supposed to have with God, which often seems abstract? This passage seems to be talking to people who want to make faith something completely cerebral—"I'm thinking right, so what does it matter what I'm actually doing?" But Paul insists that there is a real, bodily connection between Christ and the Christian. My body? I'm always trying to get it in shape, but not always in terms of its relation to Jesus. This is mysterious, and I need your guidance, Lord, to keep working on it.

"...THE FIRST OF HIS SIGNS, IN CANA OF GALILEE."

Here is the miracle, or sign, that the gospel writers call the first time that Jesus did something powerfully noticeable in public. Jesus at a party? I don't remember ever seeing this scene in stained glass! But here He is, helping people to have a great time, even maybe what we'd call too much of a good time. He shows His "glory," (though I've always found that a hard word to understand) in this act of good friendship. He is in charge of the physical world—grapes, water, alcohol content, religious paraphernalia—He's totally in control of them, not the other way around. That's probably a clue to "glory," right there.

Third Sunday after the Epiphany

Collect from *LW*: "O Lord God Almighty, because you have always supplied your servants with the several gifts that come from your Holy Spirit alone, leave us not destitute of your manifold gifts nor of grace to use them always to your honor and glory and the good of others; through Jesus Christ, your Son, our Lord, who live and reigns with you and the Holy Spirit, one God, now and forever."

MATT. 4:12-23.
"IMMEDIATELY THEY LEFT...AND FOLLOWED HIM."
This is so hard to imagine! It's funny that you can believe something without any trouble, and yet find it almost impossible to see how it could happen. These men just left everything they were doing and literally followed Jesus around the country. Most of the people I know and care about say that we're following Jesus. But I get bent out of shape if I don't do everything in my appointment book, just the way I planned. What would it take to get me to drop everything—classes, dates, schedules, church services—and follow Jesus? That's really too scary to think about, Lord. Yet I know You call me to follow You. Help me with my half-hearted attempts to let go and pursue Your way of life.

JONAH. CHAPTERS 1-4.
"THE WORD OF THE LORD CAME TO JONAH...."
One of the strangest stories in the Bible! Jonah is selected to bring God's word to people, but does everything he can to duck out of it, then finally tells the people to repent, and when they do, he's mad! Is this a story about following God? or a story about God's willingness to forgive? or about the necessity of repenting? or of God not liking reluctant prophets? or maybe God having a good laugh at people who sulk because good things happen to other people? The point, most likely, is that it's about all of the above. What does the story teach us in Epiphany? The contrast between Jonah and Jesus is a good place to start thinking about this. Whose example am I following today?

LUKE 4:14-21.

"TODAY THE SCRIPTURE HAS BEEN FULFILLED...."

OK, now this begins to hang together. Epiphany—the time when Jesus shows Himself to be following God's call to announce a new word to the people of the world. Good prophets (like Isaiah or Micah) or not-so-good prophets (like Jonah) are now the voices of the past, because now it's time to follow Jesus or not. This is the person who carries God's word because, in that baptism at the Jordan River, God said so. And now, Jesus is going around telling other people, even people in His home town, what's what. That's courage! Can I use it as an example to help me be a slightly better witness to my faith right here? On this campus? In this apartment? In my hometown? I'll need a lot of help on this one, Lord.

Week 4

Fourth Sunday After the Epiphany

Collect from *LW*: "Almighty God, because you know that
we are set among many and great dangers that by reason
of the weakness of our fallen nature we cannot always
stand upright, grant us your strength and protection to
support us in all dangers and carry us through all
temptations; through our Lord Jesus Christ, your Son, who
lives and reigns with you and the Holy Spirit, one God,
now and forever. Amen."

MICAH 6:1-8.
*"DO JUSTICE, LOVE KINDNESS AND WALK HUMBLY WITH YOUR
GOD...."*

The sheer busyness of campus life has begun to overwhelm
me. At the beginning of the semester, I promised myself to
prioritize: that was going to be my word for the new year.
Now everything has piled up; in classes where I thought I
understood the material, this last week was suddenly way
over my head; I'm going crazy trying to be a good friend to
a person who seems to need more than I can provide; my
family needs me more just when I really need them to be
supportive. I need to get a grip on what my life is all
about, and so these words from Micah can help, if only I
don't let them be yet another demand that I can't satisfy.
At least for a minute or two, Lord, with your help I can
hear them as a simple version of priorities.

PSALM 1.

"...THEIR DELIGHT IS IN THE LAW OF THE LORD...."

More words to function like a stabilizer for my chaotic existence. I'd really like to be "like a tree planted by streams of water," just calmly doing what I am meant to do. Why does the Psalmist say that meditating on the law is a delight? Doesn't that only make you feel worse? Maybe he means that it helps to set your priorities, to focus you, to let you know where you want to be. I know that I can only do that through the help of Jesus, but it is good to get centered and know where you belong. I know that's what it means to have you, Lord, watching over me. Keep watching, and I'll try to remember the delight of being where you want me to be.

I CORINTHIANS 12:27-13:13.

"...THE GREATEST OF THESE IS LOVE."

What a great reading this one is—I should read it every day and it would keep me going! I'm trying so hard to be something, to use my gifts, to make the most of these opportunities. But the more excellent way is to learn to grow in love. In this, I really still understand "as a child." But I want to learn better. I want to learn how, as a student and friend and child and teammate—or eventually as a nurse or lawyer or pastor or father or CEO or anything—how to be a person who is an expert in love. There isn't a course in it, and this kind of learning seems to be shoved under everything else, but I really want it. Help me, Lord, to be the best person at loving that I can be.

Fifth Sunday After the Epiphany

Collect from *LW*: "O God, our loving Father, through the grace of your Holy Spirit you plant the gifts of your love into the hearts of your faithful people. Grant to your servants soundness of mind and body, so that they may love you with their whole strength and with their whole heart do these things that are pleasing in your sight; through Jesus Christ, your Son, our Lord, who lives and reigns with you and the Holy Spirit, one God, now and forever. Amen."

MATT. 5:13-20.
"...NOT TO ABOLISH BUT TO FULFILL."

Jesus gets pretty direct in this part of the Sermon on the Mount. The verses before these are the ones I hear more often—"blessed are the poor in spirit...," etc. Now he's talking about fulfilling the law, about how that "rightness" will get to be the whole picture. The rightness that the law of God talks about is not just going to disappear, but Jesus' arrival in the world is going to make it become the whole environment. Sometimes I find it hard to believe that Jesus was successful; the world's capacity for rightness looks just as fragile as ever. What is this "kingdom of heaven" anyway? He talks about it as though it were right now; I tend to think of it as some distant future. Let your kingdom come, Lord, right now and also in your good, sweet time!

I COR. 9:16-23.
"I...AM UNDER CHRIST'S LAW."

Now Paul writes about the law, and what it means to be "under Christ's law." That is an expression that could identify a Christian, and the purpose of being under that law is so that I can be close enough to others that my life will help them to recognize God's action in Jesus. Because when I am living that way, then the law, the "rightness" that God wants for the world, will be clear to everyone. That's why I want to live so that people will want to know my motivations, and knowing them, will want to know about my faith. But, if that's what I want, why is it so hard to make it work? Why do I find it so easy to be angry or lazy or spiteful or envious, and so hard to be loving and contented and trusting? Guide me and shape me, O God, that Christ becomes the law that rules my heart.

LUKE 5:1-11.

"...YOU WILL BE CATCHING PEOPLE."

Jesus himself tried everything to explain to people what He was doing, and what His followers should do—make God's idea for the world real and meaningful for everyone. Here He tries something pretty spectacular. He's here to change the way we think of ourselves in the world. We're not here to persuade God that we're good enough. We're here to receive from God way more than we think we're entitled to, way more than we expect. And then, we're supposed to go and "catch" others into this same understanding. Here in Epiphany we try to "get" what Jesus' mission is, and, when we get it, we've got to spread it around. And we can do it in our everyday work. Mine isn't catching fish, it's learning systems and formulas and techniques. Can I use my work as a way to explain Jesus mission? Like Peter, my first response is, "No way! that's not for me!" Help me to get past that first response, Lord.

Celebrating Lives of Faith

(the following usually fall during Epiphany)

January 15
Martin Luther King, Jr.

"As we remember the faithful commitment of Dr. Martin Luther King, Jr., give us also we pray, O Lord,

Attentiveness to pain and oppression that others in your world are experiencing;

Perspective for discerning your concerns for troubled and neglected people;

Courage to stand supportively with those in need;

Tenderness in the care of children;

Strength to resist the temptation to turn away; and

Joy to know you are at our side in our striving to be faithful. **Amen.**"

Karl Lutze

January 18
The confession of St. Peter (January 18) to the conversion of St. Paul (January 25)

Almighty God: you have given to us Christians the greatest of all examples in the lives of your servants, Peter and Paul. We can see in them our own failures; help us also to see and follow their passion for your truth, their courage, their faithfulness. Give us grace to know all Christians as our fellow disciples, and to pray as Peter and Paul did for the well-being of your Church. Amen.

January 25
St. Paul

O THE DEPTH OF THE RICHES AND WISDOM AND KNOWLEDGE OF GOD! HOW UNSEARCHABLE ARE HIS JUDGMENTS AND HOW INSCRUTABLE HIS WAYS!

FOR WHO HAS KNOWN THE MIND OF THE LORD? OR WHO HAS BEEN HIS COUNSELOR?

OR WHO HAS GIVEN A GIFT TO HIM, TO RECEIVE A GIFT IN RETURN? FOR FROM HIM AND THROUGH HIM AND TO HIM ARE ALL THINGS. TO HIM BE THE GLORY FOREVER. AMEN.

Romans 11:33-36 NRSV

February 5
The martyrs of Japan

MY GOD, MY GOD, WHY HAVE YOU FORSAKEN ME?
WHY ARE YOU SO FAR FROM HELPING ME, FROM THE
WORDS OF MY GROANING?
O MY GOD, I CRY BY DAY, BUT YOU DO NOT ANSWER; AND
BY NIGHT, BUT FIND NO REST.
YET YOU ARE HOLY, ENTHRONED ON THE PRAISES OF
ISRAEL.
IN YOU OUR ANCESTORS TRUSTED; THEY TRUSTED, AND
YOU DELIVERED THEM.
TO YOU THEY CRIED, AND WERE SAVED; IN YOU THEY
TRUSTED, AND WERE NOT PUT TO SHAME.

Psalm 22:1-5 NRSV

February 18
Martin Luther

Behold, Lord, an empty vessel that needs to be filled. My
Lord, fill it. I am weak in the faith, strengthen me. I am
cold in love; warm me and make me fervent that my love
may go out to my neighbor. O Lord, help me. Strengthen
my faith and trust in You.

With me, there is an abundance of sin; in You is the
fullness of righteousness. Therefore I will remain with
You, from whom I can receive, but to whom I may not give.
Amen.

February 20
Rasmus Jensen

"I give you thanks dear Lord for the example of your
servant Rasmus. In the midst of journey, in search of the
Northwest passage, he paused to lead his fellow sailors in
worship of you, who guide all our travel. May I, too,
pause in the midst of my life's journey, taking my bearings
from you and trusting to you my safe passage until I am at
home in you. Amen."

L. DeAne Lagerquist

Special Days

The Baptism of Our Lord
(First Sunday after the Epiphany)

Collect from *LBW*: "Father in heaven, at the baptism of
Jesus in the River Jordan you proclaimed Him your beloved
Son and anointed Him with the Holy Spirit. Make all who
are baptized into Christ faithful in their calling to be your
children and inheritors with Him of everlasting life;
through your Son, Jesus Christ our Lord, who lives and
reigns with you and the Holy Spirit, one God, now and
forever. Amen."

reading: Mark 1:9-11. "You are my Son, the Beloved."

Meditation

The baptism of Jesus in the Jordan River, at the hands of
John the Baptist (who was not a Baptist in the modern
sense; he was, in fact Jewish)—the baptism of Jesus in the
Jordan River is the inaugural event in the public ministry of
Jesus. From there he would go forth to begin proclaiming:
"The Kingdom of God is at hand." But now for a moment
another voice speaks, the voice of His Father in heaven,
"You are my Son, the Beloved."

We commemorate and celebrate this moment each year on
the First Sunday after the Epiphany, a day on which it has
also become customary among us to remember and
celebrate our own baptism into Christ. Back sometime, for
many of us in infancy, that water was poured upon us, "In
the name of the Father and of the Son and of the Holy
Spirit." From that moment on, we say, God claimed us as
His child.

But something more was happening in our baptism. St. Paul
in the book of the Acts of the Apostles is seen affirming the
fact that all of humankind are children of God. Then who
needs baptism to give what we already possess? Or is there

something more going on? Yes, there is something more, for the claim that God puts upon us is that from the moment of our baptism we have been assigned the identity of Jesus. "You, now, are Jesus to me," God is saying. "And I have great plans for you. Watch Him and find out what they are."

Hymn Stanza

I BIND UNTO MYSELF TODAY THE STRONG NAME OF THE TRINITY
MY INVOCATION OF THE SAME, THE THREE IN ONE AND ONE IN THREE.

I BIND THIS DAY TO ME FOREVER, BY POW'R OF FAITH, CHRIST'S INCARNATION,
HIS BAPTISM IN THE JORDAN RIVER, HIS CROSS OF DEATH FOR MY SALVATION,
HIS BURSTING FROM THE SPICED TOMB, HIS RIDING UP THE HEAV'NLY WAY,
HIS COMING AT THE DAY OF DOOM, I BIND UNTO MYSELF TODAY.

St. Patrick 372-466

Closing Prayer

O God, after what happened to your Son Jesus in the Jordan River, no water can ever be the same. Let the water that flows through our daily lives, from the morning shower to a quick glassful at bedtime, be a continual reminder of the waters of our baptism that connect us to your Son. Hold us as your beloved ones, and give us courage to go forth in His name, Jesus to our world, to heal, to forgive, to proclaim good news, dying and rising. In His name we pray. Amen.

Transfiguration
(Last Sunday Before Ash Wedesday)

Collect from *LBW*: "Almighty God, on the mountain you showed your glory in the transfiguration of your Son. Give us the vision to see beyond the turmoil of our world and to behold the king in all his glory; through your Son, Jesus Christ our Lord, who lives and reigns with you and the Holy spirit, one God, now and forever. Amen."

reading: Mark 9:2-9. "Master, it is good for us to be here."

Meditation

Peter's words are typical of human reactions to the divine—both these words and the next. Peter wants to make something of his own in which to shelter and keep what he has seen. He uses the practices that he knows, because building these "booths," or temporary shelters, was a time-honored way of marking a religious experience. But it's not very far off from us either, is it, with our habit of making traditions, shrines, markers, crosses, rituals—things that will help us keep the moment.

But what is it we want to keep? God is dynamic; can we keep a burning bush? a pillar of cloud? Jesus knows both the human tendency of Peter, and the changing mystery of God. When we stay with Jesus, we know that He will continue to insist that we move along with Him, away from what we have already seen, away from what is comfortable and familiar. Building shrines on the mountain is not central to the mission, but moving ahead to the cross in Jerusalem is. What marks Jesus as the beloved Son is not that He is enshrined on a mountaintop, but that He is willing to take the cross. Standing here, we are asked if we are ready to follow Him on that path, or whether we will stay with our own constructions on the mountain.

Hymn Stanza

OH, WONDROUS TYPE! OH, VISION FAIR OF GLORY THAT
THE CHURCH MAY SHARE, WHICH CHRIST UPON THE
MOUNTAIN SHOWS, WHERE BRIGHTER THAN THE SUN HE
GLOWS!

WITH MOSES AND ELIJAH NIGH TH' INCARNATE LORD
HOLDS CONVERSE HIGH, AND FROM THE CLOUD, THE
HOLY ONE BEARS RECORD TO THE ONLY SON.

AND FAITHFUL HEARTS ARE RAISED ON HIGH BY THIS
GREAT VISION'S MYSTERY;
FOR WHICH IN JOYFUL STRAINS WE RAISE, THE VOICE OF
PRAYER, THE HYMN OF PRAISE!

(LBW #80)

Closing Prayer

Mighty God, thank you for the glorious moments when I
feel the full power of your presence, but keep me aware
that the hard work of discipleship is each day's ordinary
tasks. Give me the grace, Lord, to let go of what I think
should be celebrated and held onto in the faith. Keep me
on that walk with Jesus, even if it is going down the
mountain I'd like to stay on. In Christ's name. Amen.

Prayers of the Season

Starting another semester

Here we go again, God. Dare I mention that the break was too short? Nevertheless, it is good to be back. This is my vocation, God. It's where I belong at this point in my life. It's where you have put me. Help me not forget that, as I grit my teeth and wade into campus life and academic responsibilities once more. Keep my eyes open to what you are accomplishing in me during these years. Shape me for ventures ahead, and open those doors that lead into your future. Amen.

Returning from off-campus studies

It's been eight long months I've been away, God, a semester and a summer devoted to special ventures and adventures. I'm still caught up in the glow of that, but I'm also feeling something of a stranger back on campus. Folks assure me that will pass, so what I pray for now is your guidance as I try to integrate my time away with my time ahead. Let what I have experienced linger in me and mature, and let it enrich all those things to which I now set my hand. Amen.

For safe travel

This weekend I'm travelling home, Lord, and I'm driving a carload of friends with me. Help me to remember that there are probably better places to show off my expertise, and so to be careful and responsible at the wheel. If you could hold off on the winter storms this weekend, I'd be grateful, but if we should be in one on the road, keep us safe and bring us there and back in a comfortable, even boring, way. Amen.

Those who support our life on campus

I take them for granted, God, but without them we would
go hungry, our buildings would be a mess, the campus
would be unsafe, and the plumbing would stop working.
Just for starters! Thank you for all those taken-for-granted
ones who keep our campus alive, Lord. And help me
convey my gratefulness to them by treating them respect,
honoring their own human struggles, and now and then
telling them I appreciate what they do. Amen.

The long days of winter

God, I'm frozen to the core! No, the heating system is not
broken, and I have been bundling up when I go outside.
But this winter has been hard and long and I feel as if my
spirit is frozen up inside of me. Everyone around me
suffers the same. Help us find a way to bring what little
warmth we each have left together in such a way that we
revive one another, and be present there with us, your
everlasting warmth kindling our hearts anew and glowing
through us upon the campus. Amen.

On the way to Morning Prayer

It's eleven o'clock, Lord. What a gift You give us each
day. Even those days I don't take advantage of it. In a
few minutes I will connect again with friends I may not
see the rest of the day. In a few minutes we will leave
the rushing world of academic life, if for just a brief time.
In a few minutes we will sing and pray, we will listen and
reflect, we will keep still, then hold each other in Your
peace. Thanks. Amen.

Demanding Prof

I don't know where this prof is getting off, God, but the demands of this class keep piling up! It's not like it's the only course I'm taking! So, I'm angry and scared! I know faculty folks sometimes have greater confidence in us than we do in ourselves, and they are not unknown to push us to limits greater than we desire or deserve. Not unlike You, Lord, if I might be so bold! So, help me hang in there and maybe do more than I think I am able. And, if need be, give me courage to talk to my prof about it. Amen.

Diversity

How could I ever have imagined, O God, that You were not great enough or good enough to grace the human race with the same variety and diversity so wonderfully visible in birds and trees and the whole created order. Yet part of me remains anxious and uncomfortable around people different from me. That's not what You intended. You intended us to be a blessing upon each other. Open me to receive the blessing others can bring me, especially in their being other than I am. And make me a blessing to them. Amen.

Chicken soup season

I'm not going to die from this, Lord, but I feel lousy and weary and it's affecting the things I have to get done. And everyone else seems to have it, too, whatever it is. It must be the season. I think I need permission to take care of myself, God, and I know You give me that, and to seek some assistance if I need. So now I'm asking for strength and endurance, a little time to rest, and a bowl of chicken soup. Amen.

From the Chapel

For many years, Lutheran congregations throughout the nation have given generous support to Valparaiso University through observing "Valpo Sunday," usually in early February. The campus often observes this Sunday as well. This sermon comes from Valpo Sunday in February of 1984.

Power and Light

1 Corinthians 2:1-5
Matthew 5:13-20

"Our Scripture readings today, and many other statements of Jesus, the evangelists, and the apostles, crystallize the new attitude of mind and heart that characterizes those who join Jesus in building the kingdom of God, a kingdom that exists in the hearts of children and young people, men and women, which knows no barriers of class, nation, race, or culture. Of course this is quite revolutionary. This is why, as Jesus often said, we need to start again as little children (which is what 'conversion' means) and why we need to change our whole outlook (which is what 'repentance' means). At first sight, this call to life in the kingdom can be disturbing. We would prefer that Jesus would simply endorse our best feelings and give us a little more truth to help us on our way. He does in fact endorse all that is good and true in our thinking and aspirations, but he tells us that a new quality of living is manifested when we live as His people and spread His kingdom. His emphasis is not on 'being good' but on *following His way, through the gifts of His spirit.* The goodness is purely a by-product. This may well shake us up, as it was probably meant to do. Nowhere does Jesus exhort us simply to be good, or be pure, or be honest, or be unselfish.

"Instead, Jesus says simply, again and again, 'Follow me,' which means learning a new way of living altogether. Equally disturbing, at first, is Jesus' teaching that a person's relationship with God and his or her relationship with fellow human beings are connected very closely. God's kind of love goes far beyond the limits of ordinary human

95

niceness and kindness. 'Even the despised tax collectors,' Jesus says, in effect, 'are kind—TO EACH OTHER. Your love must be the love of the Father, who is kind to the unthankful and the evil.' Jesus identified Himself with the human race, not merely with its noblest specimens but *with all humanity*—with the blind, the deaf, the dumb, the mentally deficient, the repulsively sick, the naked, the hungry and starving, the refugee, the beggar, the outcast. So also, he says, you are to do, as my people.

"This kind of loving kindness gets expressed by God's people not merely in occasional individual acts of love, but also through His people taking public policy initiatives and making use of the resources available in the social, political, and economic orders of modern society. We have said nothing thus far about Valparaiso Sunday, which is being celebrated in our congregations throughout the country today by University alumni, friends, and supporters; yet everything in our Scripture readings provides the foundation and central meaning of Valparaiso University for all its on-campus and off-campus members. The University's motto, 'In Thy Light we shall see light,' is not a mere slogan, but a commitment. Our student publications are called *Torch, Beacon,* and *Lighter* not as shibboleths or simply by way of word-association, but to signify their roles in support of the University' s purposes. These purposes include the right of learning and the light of the Gospel both shining in the singular cause of Christian higher education. This form of higher education is committed to excellence in liberal studies, to effective scholarship and learning in academic disciplines and professional fields, to the most fruitful and rewarding kind of serial, physical, and emotion development of its members, and to cultural richness on campus. All of these University activities fall short, however, if they are not moored in spiritual and moral foundations or if we make a kind of split in our minds whereby one side of us says prayers and sings hymns and worships God in special times and places while the other side of us remains cold, critical, and unloving towards the people with whom we live and whom we meet day by day. It is just this sort of split that Jesus will not have at any price.

"The purposes of Christian higher education at this place will not be accomplished if we take such interest in our own professional and career preparation, or our own pleasure, or doing our own thing, that the light of the Gospel does not blaze brilliantly here, and if our life together is not renewed by the power of Christ's Spirit.

"It is to achieve this union of human learning and spiritual life that there is a Valparaiso University. It is this union of the lamp of learning and the light of faith that is the meaning of Valparaiso Sunday and of all the days and years of the University's life as part of the 'city set on a hill that cannot be hid,' a 'city' whose members' lives shine brightly with the light of the Gospel and the illumination of true learning.

"It is this 'city' to which the University and all its members belong. The sun of righteousness has risen over our lives. We no longer belong to ourselves; we belong to the city of God, Whose light shines in the darkness. Out of thankfulness, as redeemed sons and daughters of God, a new life is growing. We need make no convulsive efforts to let this light shine; it shines of itself through the grace of God, the source of all being, power and light...through Christ, our Lord."

Robert V. Schnabel

The Epiphany season's lessons and themes lend themselves to serious reflection on our various vocations as Christian people. Valpo's preachers have traditionally held forth on this topic in their sermons and homilies. Here is a sampling of some of their thoughts, mostly from Epiphany seasons past.

The Campus as the Kingdom of God
Epiphany 4, 1979

Saint Mark 1:21-28

"Jesus and the scribes had much in common. Both of them, for example, knew about the Kingdom of God and both of them taught about the Kingdom of God. The Kingdom of God would happen when God would rule, better when he would over-rule the Romans and all the rest who oppose God and oppressed his people. God's Kingdom would come—better, would overcome—even the forces of Satan, so that every obstacle would be removed to God's sole and gracious rule.

"Some scribes could talk about that great day in glowing, vivid colors and with a heightened sense of drama, while other scribes could take even so exciting a subject and turn it into a dull lecture or boring sermon. But when Jesus stepped on the scene, he went beyond scribal teaching. For one thing, he said the Kingdom of God was at hand, that it was about to happen. That caused some stir, of course, but not as much as we might suppose. Others had said that too—and they were proved wrong.

"The really big news was not that Jesus said that Kingdom of God would soon come, but rather that in what he did the Kingdom of God was already happening. Every scribe said that some day God would come and over rule the Kingdom of the devil. Jesus came and cast out the demons.

"Do not look to distant horizons for the coming of God; look rather to him who is even now doing what the scribes can only talk about, to Jesus who embodies what he teaches, who—if you will—practices what he preaches. That is Jesus' authority. That is what is so noticeable about Jesus.

98

That is what creates such amazement among the people.

"We are not called simply to amazement or to astonishment, however. To be sure, that is a necessary first step: awe and wonder and reverence. But we are called to be followers of this Jesus in whom God comes and overcomes Satan, to be disciples of this Jesus in whom God rules and overrules all that opposes him. And to be a disciple is to receive from Jesus his authority to cast out the demons. And we are thereby called to exercise His authority in order to exhibit his authority and so to manifest His excellent glory.

"Jesus' invitation to follow Him and to share in His authority is then an invitation to look about you on campus and to see it through the eyes of Jesus—eyes that flash with the fire of indignation and anger at the demons that possess and bind, precisely because they look with compassion upon those who are thus possessed and so bound. The depth of Jesus' determination to evict the demons and the reality of His resolution to help the afflicted can only be measured at the cross. This was the price he gladly paid for His authority to cast out the demons and to liberate the possessed.

"Thus our invitation to follow Jesus and share his authority is also our invitation to share His cross. It is comparatively easy to watch Jesus exorcise a demon and to stand back and applaud this first century version of the CBS Sports Spectacular; it is harder to understand that His authority to do so grows out of His willingness to die the redemptive death; it is hardest of all for us to follow this Jesus as His disciple. So as you look about the campus, add to your ire at the demons and to your love for their victims the willingness for Christ's sake and the Gospels to lose your life. And be strengthened, be encouraged to do so by keeping an ear open to Jesus' promise that so to follow Him is to find your life in the shared life of the resurrection."

Walter E. Keller

Righteousness: Yes or No
Epiphany 6, 1981

Matthew 5:20-36

"Unless your righteousness exceeds the righteousness of the scribes and pharisees, you will never enter the kingdom of heaven."

"Christ's words in this portion of the Sermon on the Mount are quick, disturbing, clean. Coming after the exaltation of the previous verses—you are the salt of the earth, you are a city set on a hill, you are the light of the world—the words disarm us. By these words Jesus takes us abruptly from the public eye to the interior eye of discipleship. Jesus does this not because the inside, our interior piety, is more important than the outside, the world of public action. Rather Jesus brings us up sharply to move us from our distorted views of righteousness to that key passage that comes later: 'Your heavenly Father knows what you need. But seek first his kingdom and his righteousness, and all these things shall be yours as well.'

"How do we get from the possible despair of excelling the righteousness of the scribes and Pharisees to the impossible hope of the righteousness of God? Our answer, we believe with St. Paul in the Epistle lesson for the day, is in Christ our Lord. He is our righteousness. We live by the righteousness of his faith, by his cross, his resurrection, his life in us. Without him we futilely seek to live by the law. With him we live as forgiven sinners, empowered through word and sacrament to bring the active, open, love of Christ to bear on our community.

"Our problem is the sand in our eyes. Or we hear only the rush of our own blood in our ears. Or we act only on the juices of our desires or instincts. Thus our grasp of the practical application of the Sermon on the Mount to our daily life within our communities seems sometimes so fragmentary and partial that our faith and worship gasp
for air.

"The Sermon on the Mount, writes Dietrich von Oppen, touches on more than simply the Jewish Law: 'It comes to grips with the institutional life of man as such, and in doing so it outlines a permanently valid sketch of what life actually involves: protection of life, preservation of marriage, confirmation of the pledged word, appropriate punishment for any breach of the rules, mutual obligation, exclusion of the outsider, public scrutiny of behavior within the community, reciprocal surveillance, ownership of property, and work as a means of livelihood.'

"And because Jesus seeks to take us to the actual reality behind the rules, away from public scrutiny, he wishes to place us in a new force field where you and I are addressed as individuals by the living God who revealed himself in the law so that the quality of life in the community and the love in that community may be filled with light and salt.

"Our predicament here before this portion of the text is something like the story told of the first Queen Elizabeth of England. As she grew older and more seasoned in her exercise of power and her familiarity with regal glory, she recognized the great gaps between what she was as a human being and the significant role she played as English monarch. Wishing to be honest with herself, she had her private chamber completely covered with mirrors. There she saw herself as she was: a plain woman indeed, an aging queen, a fragile human being. Before she appeared in public she commanded that all mirrors be covered. That way she was protected both from her vanity about her office and despair about her plainness. What she could do was her work.

"With Jesus' intensifying of the law we are in that private chamber of mirrors. We see that the protection of human life depends not merely on honoring the external commands of the law, Thou shall not kill. We see that we cannot love God and hate our neighbor. Even our worship, unless it is going to be the worship of an idol, depends on that regard for the brother that sees him or her as one loved by God in his Son.

"We see that not only is the human family preserved, but for the disciple, man or woman, desire without love destroys a fundamental relationship with Christ. Discipline and constraint as well as purity of heart mark the most intimate of family structures. It is not that there shall not be desire, but that love and desire give power to that purity which obeys the Lord who says, 'You have heard that it was said, but I say to you.' In a community that remains a genuine community, integrity and honesty mark the man and woman in such a way that nothing but ourselves under God needs to be called into question because to isolate any word or moment and to speak of it as true is to call into question the whole fabric of one's life.

"This intensification of the law in Jesus own words could drive us to despair if he, the crucified King of glory, had not set our sins aside. They are nailed with him to the cross. But, if you will have it, Christ too is the curtain who covers us when we move into love and service in the community. But that usage is too static. 'I am a sinner, I am a good sinner,' said Leon Bloy. One always comes back to that. To be a forgiven sinner is never to relax the relationship between the living God and ourselves. But to be a forgiven sinner is to always have a new beginning within the limits and possibilities of a given day. In those small undertakings that mark our daily life-there we hear and obey this Christ who attends to us in His righteousness. That way we can sing the kinds of hymns we sing about conscience and consciousness free from blame, take walks to the altar with many people in this Christian community where we seek to obey and to hear God's word for us in our work, where we remain, transparent to the flame of light and glory that God gives in His son."

Warren Rubel

"Who of us faced with the simple question, 'What would be a good place to have a Lutheran university?' would answer, 'Nazareth.' Not exactly one of the crossroads of history or civilization. Besides, they didn't have any Fort Wayne nearby with a bunch of keen Lutheran laymen thinking it might be a good idea to have a Lutheran university. Nazareth was just Nazareth. Could anything good come out of Nazareth? Nothing much ever had. No famous bank robbers or murderers to boast of, let alone a naval victory or such heroic quantities of snow. Nobody from Nazareth had ever made it into the Top Ten. Nazareth had not made it into the Old Testament, or the Apocrypha or Josephus or the Talmud. Nazareth was a one-donkey nothing of a town. 'And when I want a table made, I want it straight, like we've always had tables in this town, and none of those fancy curves neither.'

"'Now Philip was from Bethsaida' and he has something to tell his friend Nathanael. That Nathanael was a good man we have on the highest possible authority, and besides we have supporting circumstantial evidence. Under a fig tree was a favorite spot for reading the Bible. Yet it is possible to read the Bible twice a day under a dozen fig trees and still miss the whole point. Indeed you can read the Bible in such a way as to disenable you from getting the point. You can read it as a manual on how to be a good man—lots of rules and models to follow. You can read it as a manual on how to be a good God. The problem with Nathanael was not that he was not a good man. The core problem with Nathanael was his theology, how God was supposed to be a good God. Nazareth on Nathanael's lips means, 'That is no way for God to be doing anything.' There are ways that are fitting for God to do things, and out of Nazareth cannot possibly be one of them, out of that nothing of a town not even mentioned in the Bible.

"The god who couldn't do anything out of Nazareth had to die, and the God who could, be born for him, and that birth was birth again for Nathanael. New God, new Nathanael, Jesus of Nazareth, Nathanael his disciple. He comes the stable way, the womb way, the Nazareth way.

"The Valpo way? We, a university crowd, are more of Wise Men than shepherds. We are expected to know the answers. We do have a little planetarium. What makes the world go, how things work, how to succeed? Power and money say the realists, love say the romantics. And with the biggest college chapel in the world, and the fig trees of our required theology we even have a pretty fair handle on God. There are standards that he has to meet, otherwise we'll flunk him out. There are ways that are fitting for Him to behave, and ways that are not. When we lay it down for God, it is ridiculous to suppose that we are than dealing with God, the living God.

"Jesus knew how ridiculous and so gave Nathanael a poke about his fig tree. With a grin? Now a grin is not something God is supposed to do, but neither is he supposed to come from Nazareth, or be born in a stable, or flee as a refugee, or make tables for the bumpkins of Nazareth the way they want their tables made.

"What's he supposed to be like? Philip does not have an argument with Nathanael. They could have had a real good one, a Biblical one, a theological one. But Philip was already a Jesus man. He knew there is nothing persuasive of Jesus better than Jesus himself. 'Philip said to him, 'Come and see.' Jesus saw Nathanael coming.' Come on, Nathaniel, 'Before Philip called you, when you were under the fig tree, I saw you.' Nathanael wasn't seeing, but he was seen by Jesus of Nazareth, yes Nazareth. The first question is not whether you believe in God but whether He believes in you. Jesus accepted Nathanael. Jesus saw Nathanael and had his man Philip say to Him, 'Come and see.' Nathanael was seen. He came and he saw Jesus of Nazareth.

"In the Gospel of John seeing is not just rods and cones work. It is that; his eyes saw the man from Nazareth, and that man came across to Nathanael, welcoming Nathanael, and Nathanael then saw be-personed-ly, and exclaimed, 'Rabbi, you are the Son of God! You are the King of Israel.' Not a very cautious or guarded way of talking, but the best that could come from him when Jesus made him his man. And then perhaps a grin. Come on, you say big words, you haven't seen anything yet. You'll see the gate of heaven, the one who knows the way (3:13) the one who is the way, the one to be lifted up. That is certainly no way for a Son of God and the King of Israel to go.

"Nathanael had called him Rabbi and Son of God and the King of Israel. Jesus picks up none of these titles, and speaks rather of the Son of man, the name that makes Him interchangeable with everyman, and any man. It is the title that Jesus uses when He speaks of His glory, the glory of the Son of man. In Holy Week Jesus said, 'The hour has come for the Son of man to be glorified,' and spoke of His death, of His being lifted up from the earth.

"Jesus kept his promise to Nathanael, 'You shall see greater things than these.' Greater than he could ever have imagined, than he wanted; he wanted no Christ that would come from Nazareth, let alone one that dies on a cross and has that as His throne, a cross by which he draws all whom He draws to Himself. There He does for us what was ours for our sin, our sin of trying to make Him into another kind of God. He is the Calvary kind, the Nazareth kind. If He can have His way the Nazareth way, the Calvary way, then perhaps by way of Valpo, too.

"We lay aside our pride and guile, our trust in ourselves as altogether fitting channels for God's working, when we pray that this may be a University 'under the cross.' That is a Nazareth prayer from Nazareth hearts, that are astonished that our Lord should see us under our fig trees, should care about us, about you, about me. Can anything good come out of Valpo, out of you, out of me? Our measuring of ourselves may not be at all encouraging. Do we judge the way the world judges? Do we judge the way natural religion judges? Do we judge with our own judgment? Do we judge with the judgment of Jesus of Nazareth? Who says Yes to us? Our Yes of pride and guile rings hollow, and yet our 'No, we really aren't worth much,' comes into contradiction with his Yes. The 'Yes you, I saw you' is spoken by the man from Nazareth.

"IF THEY MIGHT GUESS HIS BETHLEHEM OF BIRTH...
A NAZARETH NONE AFTER MAY DESPISE!
AND THERE HE DWELLS...
IN LANES OR CHAMBERS IS HIS GOSPEL ...
THE LAND'S SALVATION HIDDEN IN THE NAME
WHICH FOR HIS PILGRIMAGE IN TIME NOW HATH
OUR BODIES' HALLOWED REGION FOR HIS PATH,
WE HIS CAPERNAUM, HIS BETHANY, -BUT AH! WE TOO HIS MOUNT,
HIS CALVARY!

"His Nazareth, His Dau, His Scheele, His Brandt, His Neils, His Valparaiso. Amen."

Norman Nagel

Amy E. Kindler, March 1975

Lent

The Season of Lent

The season of Lent often has been described as a journey, and that may be as good a metaphor as any. But on campus, Lent also means the long season of hard work carried out in the dull days of an Indiana winter. We're intrigued by the idea of journey, but real life demands that we stay right here, meeting deadlines and slogging to class through the tired slush of late February. The Christian tradition stresses that the believer on the path toward Easter looks forward to that festival with longing, but we often picture spring break with more eager anticipation! Can we keep our focus on both longings, and maybe learn from both? The Biblical readings for the Lenten season focus our attention on introspection, self-examination, and readiness for trial. Like a team coach, Lent demands that we get up early in the dim hours and spend time on strength training. During so-called "spring semester," we spend a lot of time getting ready for weather we hardly can imagine and preparing for exams whose content is at present a mystery; during Lent, we work out with various forms of worship life, preparing for the always surprising celebrations of Easter.

One recurrent experience draws the campus community together during Lent, and that is the World Relief Campaign. While we're focused on the disciplines of our personal faith life—reading the Bible, praying more seriously, sacrificing certain pleasures or simply worshipping more often—we're also facing outward toward the wider world, and learning to put faith in action by providing work and money for needs around the world. The campaign, sponsored jointly for many years by the Chapel and by St. Teresa's, has helped groups of people on several continents by buying everything from cows to refrigerators to looms to water pumps and land.

Every experienced Christian finds devotional patterns that work best in personal faith development during Lent. These prayers are keyed to certain readings, and can be used throughout the weeks of Lenten observance.

Weekly Devotional Thoughts
Ash Wednesday

Collect from *LBW*: "Almighty and ever-living God, you hate nothing that you have made and you forgive the sins of all who are penitent. Create in us new and honest hearts, so that, truly repenting of our sins, we may obtain from you, the God of all mercy, full pardon and forgiveness; through your Son, Jesus Christ our Lord, who lives and reigns with you and the Holy Spirit, one God now and forever. Amen."

PSALM 51:1-13
"THOU DESIREST TRUTH IN THE INWARD PARTS...."

Everybody talks about truth, but mostly that means appearing to be truthful. It's easy to be truthful about things that don't matter much, but real honesty about myself is hard. I have to face myself without rationales, excuses—without the looks that I put on when I talk with other people. With You, God, I have to try to be myself-whatever that means. Even though I know I can't hide from You, it's my instinct to pretend that I'm more pious than I am, or more perfect, or at least that I'm trying hard, and that ought to count for something. I need to push against that instinct, because it's the root of sin, it separates me from You. Let me aim for "truth in the inward parts"—no masks and no mirrors, just the real me trying to see the real You.

Week 1.

Collect from *LBW:* "Lord God, our strength, the battle of good and evil rages within and around us, and our ancient foe tempts us with his deceits and empty promises. Keep us steadfast in your Word and, when we fall, raise us again and restore us through your son, Jesus Christ our Lord, who lives and reigns with you and the Holy Spirit, one God, now and forever. Amen."

MATTHEW 4:1-11
"HE SHALL GIVE HIS ANGELS CHARGE OVER THEE...."
I usually try to avoid situations where I have to "do without." The idea of going off into the wilderness—any wilderness—without plenty of supplies seems crazy to me. But Jesus did it, and somehow I should learn from this. What? One thing is to learn that everyday life is filled with distractions, and it's hard to concentrate on my relationship with you because I'm so busy. During Lent, let me leave out some things and concentrate on trusting you to provide what I need most.

GENESIS 22:1-18
"AND ABRAHAM SAID, "HERE AM I."
Abraham gets a clear message from you, God; it's a terrifying message, but at least it is clear. As I set out on my own Lenten journey, send me some clear messages about the path you want me to follow. I find myself often feeling like Isaac: I know that this trip is significant, but just what is my role? And every now and then, when I get a clue, the answer to my question seems to be more demanding that I am ready for. Help me to trust that I will get both the mission and the ram in the bushes—the help that I need so that I can fulfill your plans for me.

ROMANS 10: 8B-13
"HOW SHALL THEY HEAR WITHOUT A PREACHER?"

Here in middle class America, I tend to see myself as part
of the Christian world that is sent to "preach the gospel of
peace" to everybody else. But I need help in seeing that
much of the world is more Christian than we are, and that
others may indeed be reaching out to me with the good
news! Give me an open heart to receive from others who
nevertheless need something I can give. Make this year's
World Relief Campaign successful because I give myself to
it. Help me talk about it well to my friends too, so that
we can give money and still see ourselves as receiving
from others.

Week 2.

Collect from *LBW:* "Heavenly Father, it is your glory always to have mercy. Bring back all who have erred and strayed from your ways; lead them again to embrace in faith the truth of your Word and to hold it fast; through Jesus Christ your Son our Lord, who lives and reigns with you and the Holy Spirit, one God, now and forever. Amen."

JOHN 4:5-26
"HE WILL TELL US ALL THINGS...."

This woman was so lucky! She is just doing her ordinary job for the day, and it turns into a real life-saving conversation with Jesus, where she even asks questions that show how little she understands. I'd like to be that way—so involved in what's going on that I forget to protect myself and my ignorance. I'm always trying to convince people of how little I need to learn, and so I stay clueless about what really matters. For me the living water would be a sparkling stream of forgetting about myself for awhile, just soaking up the richness of your love.

ROMANS 5:1-11
"TRIBULATION WORKETH PATIENCE...."

I really do get tired of hearing about how good suffering can be for me. Not that most of my suffering is in the category that would count with serious martyrdom. I complain a lot, but I know other people who suffer more than I do. Still, my suffering feels bad to me, and I'd like to have less, not more. Why is it that religious wisdom says suffering is good, but every other kind of expert says to avoid it however I can? Help me to sort out the "tribulation" that leads to hope from the other stuff with which I have to deal.

Sometimes it seems easy to understand the metaphors that Biblical writers use, and other times they just escape into so much mist. Do I thirst for you? for a sense of your presence in my everyday life? for the splash of cold water that your truth might give to my illusions and delusions? Or do I just let those words pour out of my mouth without really meaning them at all? They're so familiar that what they could mean doesn't even impact me. But I think I could be afraid of the flood that might sweep me and my little plans away. I want to mean what I say when I pray these words; let my mind be open and active in prayer.

Week 3

Collect from *LBW*: "Eternal Lord, your kingdom has broken into our troubled world through the life, death, and resurrection of your Son. Help us to hear your Word and obey it, so that we become instruments of your redeeming love; through your son, Jesus Christ our Lord, who lives and reigns with you and the Holy Spirit, one God, now and forever. Amen."

ISAIAH 42:14-21
"I WILL MAKE DARKNESS LIGHT BEFORE THEM...."

It seems to me that the places I'm in have more darkness than light about them, no matter what they say. Here we are surrounded by the motto, "In thy light we see light," but I see an awful lot of bad stuff going on. There is just as much bickering, bad-mouthing, gossip, and character assassination here as there ever was in high school. There is racism and hatred and drunkenness and cheating, just as if we didn't even claim to be a Christian school. Most people around here don't care that it's Lent. I don't so much hear a new song as I hear plenty of the old ones, and sometimes the lyrics draw me in. Are you ever really going to do what Isaiah promises here: prevail against your enemies? Help me to be part of the light that shines within this school.

I CORINTHIANS 1:22-25
"THE FOOLISHNESS OF GOD IS WISER...."

I often think about things that could have been arranged better; at least if I'd been in charge. I'd never have made teeth, for example, or the really cold winds up on the hill around the Chapel. Of course I know that God's "foolishness" is really about apparent weakness and incapacity, about how God accomplishes what He wants to happen by using what looks like a poor strategy. If it were up to me, for instance, to spread the good news, it probably wouldn't get very far: I'm too busy, or too distracted, or too timid. Can you help me have a balance between looking honestly at my failings, and using them as an excuse for doing nothing? If I understand correctly, I am part of that "weakness" that you rely on. Use my "weakness," Lord, in ways that will further Your goals.

EXODUS 3:1-8B
"A LAND FLOWING WITH MILK AND HONEY...."
If you intend for us to be surrounded with everything we like (because I'm assuming that's what 'milk and honey' is about) then why do we always seem to be told that things we like are not good? How is it possible to sort out what's really "good" from things we just like? And if abundance is good (plenty of milk and honey), why do we try to give things up for Lent? And it is hard to understand why freedom from oppression means having plenty of what I like. Maybe my experience is just too different from the oppressed Israelites. I know that the standard way to get into these stories is to say that, like the Israelites, I'm oppressed by sin. But I feel oppressed only by minor things like crummy weather and too many deadlines. Do I have to feel truly oppressed before I can feel truly free?

Week 4

Collect from *LBW*: "God of all mercy, by your power to
heal and to forgive, graciously cleanse us from all sin and
make us strong: through your son, Jesus Christ our Lord,
who lives and reigns with you and the Holy Spirit, one
God, now and forever. Amen."

PSALM 43
"WHY ARE YOU CAST DOWN, O MY SOUL?"

If it isn't this week, then it's one of the others. Somehow
I'm not always in synch with the readings. They may be
gloomy, and I'm feeling pretty good. But I do know about
those "cast down" times. (Is a bad mood the same as your
soul being cast down?) It's really tempting to go with the
easy uppers—maybe drinking, maybe a chocolate pig-out,
maybe shopping. Everybody says, "don't stay down when
there's all this available to get you up!" But by now I know
those things won't be good for long. I should work on
getting what I really need, but I think, like the Psalm says,
it needs to come from You, gracious God. So I ask, even in
the midst of a bummer time, "Oh, send out your light and
your truth, let them lead me."

NUMBERS 21:4-9
"OUR SOUL LOATHES THIS WORTHLESS BREAD...."

This is it again—complaints about the situation. These
wanderers in the desert—those who live in northwest
Indiana in winter know how they felt—there is a great big
nothing here! And what they do have, they don't want. I
know that the library is full of great books, there are all
kinds of worthwhile lectures I could go to, the gym is full
of equipment I could use, there's morning prayer every
day, but when I'm down, none of this sounds good to me.
It's just like the bread that these people loathe. Yeah, yeah,
I know it would be good for me but I don't want it. Maybe
I need to notice that these ungrateful whiners got zapped
even by a God whose faithfulness and love endure forever.
Maybe there is a helpful lesson there for us Northwest

Indiana wanderers. Help me not to take Your good gifts for granted, Lord, especially when I'm feeling loathsome.

LUKE 15: 11-32
"THIS MY SON WAS DEAD AND IS ALIVE AGAIN...."
Getting back up after being down is something so great that there should be a huge party for it, but though no one else is noticing, at least I can be thankful in front of you, Lord. Even if I wasn't rolling around with the pigs, I was feeling pretty bad. The way my life goes back and forth, or up and down, I guess it's just part of being human. This great story from Jesus about the son who storms off thinking he has it all together tells me something new every time I read it, and this time, I'm thinking how incredibly thankful he has to be while he's sitting there with his father, back where he belongs. Thanks, Lord, for bringing me back to that table, time after time.

Week 5

Collect from *LBW*: "Almighty God, our redeemer, in our weakness we have failed to be your messengers of forgiveness and hope in the world. Renew us by your Holy Spirit, that we may follow your commands and proclaim your reign of love, through your son, Jesus Christ our Lord, who lives and reigns with you and the Holy Spirit, one God, now and forever. Amen."

EZEKIEL 37: 1-3
"...CAN THESE BONES LIVE?"

Journeys for Lent might be easier to concentrate on if there weren't all this other stuff going on. Advertising is all about "spring" this and "spring" that, and I can even begin to see signs that an actual spring even might happen here. Meanwhile, in worship, we go into this "dry bones" mode and try to feel that the world is empty and used up. Where do I really belong? I want to be completely into the Lenten journey, but what about real life? Where does this valley of dry bones exist—is it me and my classmates, or what I have to imagine?

JOHN 12: 20-23
"...WE WISH TO SEE JESUS."

Interesting. I was asking about what I see, and in this reading, the single thing these men want to see is—Jesus. That's what I need to keep central: where do I see Jesus? Sometimes it seems to me that I only see Him on Sunday when I go to church, where I can try to focus. But I know it's true that I am supposed to see Him in the faces and actions of fellow Christians. That's a stretch! Most impossible of all, I'm supposed to see Jesus when I look in the mirror! Lord, I need a lot of help trying to see Jesus when I look around in this world. Give me the eyes of faith that can really see Jesus in the best and worst of situations.

"...I PRESS FORWARD TOWARD THE GOAL...."

Everybody is obsessing about goals. We're encouraged in class today to take a look at the course goals in the syllabus. My friends who are seniors are doing resumes, and they're really into thinking about life goals. The fraternity/sorority is doing a self-assessment, and we're supposed to be writing our goals to see if they match the mission. My goal is just to get to the weekend and do my laundry. But the real, true goal—it's up there ahead of us in the next weeks, and it isn't pretty. If I'm shaping my life by this Lenten journey, then the goal is Golgotha, and believing that something good lies on the other side. I'd rather go around by some other route, if it's all the same to you, Lord. But I guess it isn't, and that's the point.

Holy Week

Sunday of the Passion
(Also known as Palm Sunday)

Collect from *LBW*: "Almighty God, you sent your Son, our Savior Jesus Christ, to take our flesh upon Him and to suffer death on the cross. Grant that we may share in His obedience to your will and in the glorious victory of His resurrection; through your son, Jesus Christ our Lord, who lives and reigns with you and the Holy Spirit, one God, now and forever. Amen."

MARK 14: 1-15
"WHAT THIS WOMAN HAS DONE WILL BE TOLD AS A MEMORIAL TO HER...."

Here's another one of those stories from the Bible where a person does something completely over the top, something so extravagant and absolute that there doesn't seem to be any way that I can follow the example. This woman buys the most expensive present anybody can buy and pours it all out as a tribute to Jesus. Well, that kind of behavior just seems bizarre to me. What is it supposed to mean for my life? Maybe the only thing to do with it is to do what Jesus said—just tell it in praise of her great devotion. Period. She's out of my league. But that's all right; I'll keep trusting that there's room for both of us in your purposes, Lord.

Wednesday in Holy Week

Collect from *LBW*: "Almighty God, your Son our Savior suffered at the hands of men and endured the shame of the cross. Grant that we may walk in the way of His cross and find it the way of life and peace; through your Son, Jesus Christ our Lord. Amen."

ROMANS 5: 6-11
"WHILE WE WERE STILL SINNERS...."

This is a week when I hardly know where I am, Lord. There's such a pushing and shoving in my world that it's hard to know where to look or what to do or feel. School work demands more time than ever, yet looking forward to an Easter holiday is on everybody's mind. Family wants me to come home for R & R; people want me to stay here at Valpo for a lot of worship services—I don't know what to do. There is comfort in this reading, though, knowing that you accomplish your purposes even when—as sinners—we don't seem to know what we're doing. Get me into the spirit for this week, and help me to be the blessing that this spirit promises.

Maundy Thursday

Collect from *LBW*: "Holy God, source of all love, on the night of His betrayal, Jesus gave His disciples a new commandment: To love one another as He had loved them. By your Holy Spirit write this commandment in our hearts; through your son, Jesus Christ our Lord, who lives and reigns with you and the Holy Spirit, one God, now and forever. Amen."

JOHN 13:1-17, 34
"A NEW COMMANDMENT I GIVE YOU, THAT YOU LOVE ONE ANOTHER...."

How can love be on Jesus' mind during this horrible time in His life? He knows that His death is coming soon and that he is being abandoned by all His friends. He knows the feeling of complete loss of everything—yet here He is focused on love. So this is not just mushy sweet feelings, like a cheap greeting card, but instead it is love that I'm only just beginning to learn about—hard love, serious love, love that means work and promises and commitment. Sometimes not very far at all from death, since it seems to mean putting my self and my desires second to the needs of others. But knowing that kind of love is important, and I want to learn it better. Make my worship during this time of the Passion Week a learning experience in love.

Good Friday

Collect from *LBW*: "Lord Jesus, you carried our sins in your own body on the tree so that we might have life. May we and all who remember this day find new life in you now and in the world to come, where you live and reign with the Father and the Holy Spirit, now and forever. Amen."

PSALM 22: 1-23
"FROM MY MOTHER'S WOMB YOU HAVE BEEN MY GOD...."
I'm trying to imagine what it would be like to feel that you had abandoned me, Lord. You are familiar, so much a part of who I am, like my eyes or my hair or my skin. I do not want to lose you, to feel the terrible, ultimate sadness of your absence. Jesus on the cross felt that—the worst loss imaginable—and I believe that He felt it in my place, so that I would not have to experience it. As I think about His experience, deepen my gratitude for this gift to me. But only by knowing the possibility of its loss can I fully realize what the gift means. And Good Friday gives me some faint picture of what the loss of your presence would be.

Celebrating Lives of Faith

(the following usually fall during Lent:)

March 1
George Herbert, priest and poet (1632)

> COME, MY WAY, MY TRUTH, MY LIFE:
> SUCH A WAY AS GIVES US BREATH;
> SUCH A TRUTH AS ENDS ALL STRIFE;
> SUCH A LIFE AS CONQUERS DEATH.
>
> COME, MY LIGHT, MY FEAST, MY STRENGTH:
> SUCH A LIGHT AS SHOWS A FEAST;
> SUCH A FEAST AS MENDS IN LENGTH;
> SUCH A STRENGTH AS MAKES HIS GUEST.
>
> COME MY JOY, MY LOVE, MY HEART:
> SUCH A JOY AS NONE CAN MOVE;
> SUCH A LOVE AS NONE CAN PART;
> SUCH A HEART AS JOYS IN LOVE.

LBW #513. Text by George Herbert, 1593-1632

March 7
Thomas Aquinas, teacher of the faith

Almighty God, you made Thomas Aquinas known for the wisdom of his teaching and holiness of life. I give thanks to you for the gifts of grace that enabled him to lead others to a fuller knowledge and understanding of the truth seen in your Son Jesus Christ my Lord. Amen.

March 17
Patrick, Bishop, missionary to Ireland (461)

"Lord of journeys, we thank you for Abraham and Sarah
who walked in faith to a land they could not see. We
thank you for Moses and Miriam who led our people from
a land of bondage to a place of freedom. We thank you
for bringing a French slave named Patrick to Ireland,
where he learned to love your people, and where he
returned to preach your Gospel and turn many into your
ways. Teach us the virtues of Holy Patrick and of Irish
people—deep learning, generous hospitality, affable humor,
and-that we need to make our own journeys in you
footpaths. Amen."

Edward M. Gaffney

March 19
Joseph, guardian of Jesus

Lord God, you announce yourself to us as father, and yet
the image of father can be hard for us today. We want to
be what is best about fathers. Let Joseph's willingness to
protect the helpless be our model. May our fathers be
celebrated for their strength on behalf of others, their
modesty, their persistence, their wisdom in seeking
alternate paths to safety, their openness to angelic
messages of mercy and kindness. Amen.

March 22
Jonathan Edwards, teacher and missionary to the American Indians

O God, Shepherd of my soul, I thank you for your servant
Jonathan Edwards whom you called to preach the Gospel
to the American Indians. Continue to raise up courageous
teachers and preachers to herald the unsearchable riches
of your grace given through the suffering, death and
resurrection of my Savior Jesus Christ who with you and
the Holy Spirit are ever one God, now and forever. Amen.

Special Days

Annunciation of our Lord

Prayer of the Day from *LW*: "We implore you, O Lord, to pour forth your grace on us that, as we have known the incarnation of your Son Jesus Christ by the message of the angel, so by His cross and Passion we may be brought to the glory of His resurrection; through our Lord Jesus Christ, who lives and reigns with you and the Holy Spirit, one God, now and forever. Amen."

Reading: 1:26-38 ... you will conceive in your womb... and you will name him Jesus.

Meditation

Within Gloria Christi Chapel resides a beautiful icon created by Nicolas of Argyropolis in 1889. When originally received by the University, its vibrant colors and exquisite detail were hidden by decades of residue from incense and candle suet. Now fully restored, the message of Gabriel is clearly visible as the messenger is depicted greeting the Blessed Virgin Mary with news of an immaculate conception and a gift of roses. Worshipers and visitors alike are reminded of this often-dismissed event when gazing upon this holy image of news that initiate the culmination of the world's salvation. "God of God and light of light" confines Himself to the darkness of a womb in order that the incomprehensible might come to humanity as bone of our bone and flesh of our flesh. God becomes fully human! In this human body God embodies our sin, is placed in earth's womb, a tomb, only to break forth from its darkness to take up life again. Darkness can not contain this heavenly light for long. And in His light we see light!

Hymn Stanza

THE ANGEL GABRIEL FROM HEAVEN CAME,
WITH WINGS AS DRIFTED SNOW, WITH EYES AS FLAME;
"ALL HAIL TO THEE, O LOWLY MAIDEN MARY,
MOST HIGHLY FAVORED LADY." GLORIA!

"FOR KNOW A BLESSED MOTHER THOU SHALT BE,
ALL GENERATIONS LAUD AND HONOR THEE;
THY SON SHALL BE EMMANUEL, BY SEERS FORETOLD,
MOST HIGHLY FAVORED LADY." GLORIA!   WOV #632

Closing Prayer

Pour your grace into my heart O God, that believing in
your word I may receive Christ daily unto myself and by
my life make known the wonder of your love through
Jesus Christ my Lord. Amen.

Good Friday

Collect from *LBW*: "Almighty God, we ask you to look with mercy on your family, for whom our Lord Jesus Christ was willing to be betrayed and to be given over to the hands of sinners and to suffer death on the cross; who now lives and reigns with you and the Holy spirit, one God, now and forever. Amen."

reading: Isaiah 52:13-53:12. "...wounded for our transgressions...."

Meditation

Perhaps it would be better just to read these words and sit in silence with them. Our thoughts on this subject tend to swirl around and veer off into something else. It may be that our emotions at this hour can take only so much concentration on the subject in front of us. Looking at Jesus on the cross has to move us to pity or shock or horror or sorrow, but we may also sit in numbness.

After all, we live in a world with so much violence, so many innocent deaths, so many victims. We've seen TV pictures of things as bad as a crucifixion, so that just the visual image is hardly stunning any more. But Isaiah's words make it clear—this death is for you! If the horror of the scene itself has lost some of its power, those words have a power to chill the heart—this is my fault! my ugly temper, my lies, my lust, my cruel words, my cheating, my cold superiority. All of us can fill out the list until it is endless, and then we understand that simply to be human is to have caused this disaster. We're implicated just because we're breathing. Unless this story has an ending better than its beginning, we're lost. We're really in need of the next chapter.

Hymn Stanza

SACRED HEAD, NOW WOUNDED, WITH GRIEF AND SHAME
BOWED DOWN;
NOW SCORNFULLY SURROUNDED, WITH THORNS THINE
ONLY CROWN
SACRED HEAD, WHAT GLORY, WHAT BLISS TILL NOW
WAS THINE!
YET, THOUGH DESPISED AND GORY, I JOY TO CALL
THEE MINE.

WHAT LANGUAGE SHALL I BORROW TO THANK THEE,
DEAREST FRIEND,
FOR THIS THY DYING SORROW, THY PITY WITHOUT END?
OH, MAKE ME THINE FOREVER, AND SHOULD I FAINTING BE
LORD, LET ME NEVER, NEVER OUTLIVE MY LOVE TO THEE.

(LBW #116)

Closing Prayer

Keep fresh in my vision and my heart, Lord, the sense of
my involvement with you. Let me feel this closeness here
at this moment with true sorrow and repentance, and
then give me the joy that comes in sharing your victory
also. Be with all victims of violence, give them the comfort
of knowing your presence, and bring them through their
sufferings to victory over pain and hatred. For the sake of
Jesus who suffered for victim and perpetrator. Amen.

Prayers of the Season

Beginning of Lent

"When over silent wint'ry earth new promise grows
And hearts delight in what eyes cannot see,
Then into dusty well-worn paths our footsteps press
To follow once again from Galilee.
Come sun, your growing warmth bestow!
Can frozen hearts with courage grow
To follow where the Savior leads?"

(From "Paschal Hymn," David H. Kehret)

World Relief Campaign

I come to you, Lord, in trust that you will send real help to
me and to my friends who are also feeling this way. We are
spending a lot of energy finding out about this distant place
with many needs, and the more I find out, the more
confused and guilty and sad I get. How is the world
organized that some have much, and some have little? Help
us to raise the money, but also help us gain some peace of
mind over this. Give more people just some of our
commitment, and bless everyone who is involved with the
project. Amen.

Going on service trip

I'm excited, but also nervous. My roommate is going to
Florida, and I sometimes wish I were going to do that,
too—mostly because I'd know what to expect. Make me
braver, Lord, about going out of my comfort zone. I know
this is a good thing to do, and I want to do it with my whole
heart. Thanks for my friends—even the ones who talked me
into this—and keep us safe while we have a great time. Amen.

Team trips

Being a part of this team, Lord, is one of the great blessings
of my life. I don't always remember that, because often I'm
focused on other things about team effort. But I will never
forget it, and I want my memories to be of good things. Help
me to remember that when I'm tempted to be less than you
want me to be. Give us all the strength to play at our best,
and give us that edge that will help us win. Amen.

Going home

Thank you, Lord, for this break, because I'm really tired of being at school. Classes seem to be stalled at this point, and the last round of exams seemed like just so much pointless effort. I need to have my energy charged up, and maybe being at home will do that. Help me with the job search, and give me patience with those little things that bother me, so that I remember to be grateful for the good things at home. Bring me back to school with some restored excitement about what I'm doing. Amen.

Heading for fun

Maybe there are some people who think that if I bring You into it, Lord, I'm guaranteeing that I can't have fun on this trip. But Jesus apparently partied, and didn't stop people from having a good time. I want to relax and enjoy myself, but I also want to feel good afterwards about what I've done. Help me find that balance, and keep me—whatever I'm doing—the person I know You want me to be. Amen.

Touring with musical group

We're almost ready for this trip—that is, the music is almost learned— but I am really ready! Our program is beautiful, and it makes me proud to be part of a group that can present such a wonderful concert. Keep us safe on the road, Lord, and give us the good spirits to get along with each other, even through the problems and glitches that will happen. Let me remember that my gifts come from You, even those that I have spent long hours improving, and so let me make music as a way to thank You for those gifts. Amen.

Lining up a summer job

With all I have to attend to over the next weeks, God, I don't want to worry beyond them, but I must. Summer jobs don't just happen. Hear the ill-expressed cries of my heart (money, change of pace, location, experience) and open the doors that You want me to walk through. I'll do my part filling out applications. Amen

From the Chapel

Living In and Out of Baptism
(a Lenten Catechetical Homily)

"The focus of our discipline these 40 days of Lent is the Christian faith and life. We are concerned for repentance, for faith, and for a holy life. Our guide is the catechism. Tonight, baptism—as what we live in and out of.

"Baptism is about who you are, about where you are. It is about your being saved, forgiven, freed from death and devil. It is about being brought from death to life, and that 'in Christ.' It is about the anchor the gospel has in your life, or, better, about the anchor your life has in the gospel. It is about the death of your otherwise death-bound life. It is about your being the church of Jesus Christ. It is about how you live each day of the rest of your life.

"All of that is really saying only one thing: baptism is the life-changing, acted-out promise of God that changes what or who or where you are. And if that is at all true in any way (and we Christians are the ones who stake our life on the risk that it is finally, ultimately, really true), then that says volumes about the daily grind!

"And we know about the daily grind! The paper work has piled up. Students work feverishly to do their assigned tasks. Faculty and staff do as well, and they go to countless meetings, too, so they can worry about everything and anything connected with being 'a University under the cross.'

"In countless ways known only to ourselves alone, we worry about ourselves—our worth, our health, our career, our future. All this, because at bottom we worry (however we might say it) about God—whether God can be trusted, whether the world is at all a safe place in which to live, whether we'll make it finally, whether we can do enough to hold back the rushing tide of chaos long enough to amount to something, whether there's a fig leaf big enough to hide

132 to something, whether there's a fig leaf big enough to hide

our shame at being anything but who and what and where we're meant to be.

"What is a little water against all that? How can water produce such great effects as forgiveness, deliverance, salvation? 'It is not the water that produces these effects, but the Word of God connected with the water, and our faith that relies on the Word of God connected with the water.'

"The Word is the promise of God that this ritual washing is in fact God's own doing. It's effective, not because it's a real and not a ritual washing—for it is clearly a ritual washing! It is effective because 'God himself stakes his honor, his power, and his might on it. Therefore it is not simply a natural water, but a divine, heavenly, holy, and blessed water....' Water is water is water. But when God stakes his honor on it, then things happen. The promise is forgiveness, deliverance from death, and salvation. That much!

"It matters—for our world of worrying and agonizing about the weighty matters of life...and death. It matters for the change, the second birth, that it 'does.' The catechism says it this way:

"It signifies that the old Adam in us, together with all sins and evil lusts, should be drowned by daily sorrow and repentance and be put to death, and that the new man should come forth daily and rise up, cleansed and righteous, to live forever in God's presence.

"It matters daily, not just back there in the deep recesses of our unconscious memory. It matters daily, for our sorrow and repentance—so that our sorrow may not be empty grief, but a holy dying with Christ, as we suffer the loss of all things so as to be found in him. It matters daily, by anchoring us in the cross of Jesus, putting us to death with Him, so that Paul can say that we were 'co-buried'

133

with Christ, 'co-crucified' with Christ, 'co-dead' with Christ, and thus 'co-living' with Christ.

"It matters daily, so that 'in baptism every Christian has enough to study and to practice' all life long. It matters daily, so that we may 'draw strength and comfort from it when our sins or conscience oppress us, and we (may) retort, 'But I am baptized!' It matters daily, because repentance and faith are our daily need, 'actions (that) must continue in us our whole life long.' It matters daily, because baptism is the whole Christian life in miniature. It matters daily, because rescue from death is a real need in our daily, death-bound life. It matters daily, for it locates us (Adam, where are you?) within the community of people who like us have been broken off from the world of death and marked with the sign of the cross for life.
It matters daily, to deliver us from the bind we're in, from the narrows and tight spots into the large space of the freedom of the children of God. It matters daily, for it provides us a place from which to view the world no longer as chaos but as cosmos, and to do so as people who have become God's agents for opposing and doing in the chaos. It matters daily, to enable us to say, 'I am not alone; I am in the community of the rescued rescuers.'

"Baptism overcomes death because it overcomes the barrier of time by tying us to the death and resurrection of Jesus. Baptism grants life because it overcomes the barrier of space by tying us into the body of Christ, the Church.

"So you may use your baptism, when each morning you greet the new day with the sign of the dear holy cross and the remembrance of your baptism 'in the Name of the Father and of the Son and of the Holy Spirit.'

"You may use your baptism when you do what your vocation calls for you to do, as a freed and forgiven person, as one whose life depends on God's watery word, and not on your work. You may use your baptism when, in your life style, you get to reflect and exemplify the new 'way' of life in Christ—forgiving, just as you have been forgiven. You may use—live in, and live out of—your baptism when, at day's end and at life's end, you retire at peace, and say of your work what God says about His own creation, 'That's good!' You may use—live in, and live out of—your baptism when in the face of all contrary appearances, in the teeth of pain and suffering and especially death, in spite of all life's dilemmas and ambiguities, and in contrast to all grief and all anxiety, you nevertheless live, really live.

"'We were buried with Christ by baptism into death, so that as Christ was raised from the dead by the glory of the Father, we too might walk, in newness of life.' Newness of life—in the Name of the Father and of the Son and of the Holy Spirit."

David G. Truemper

Pilate Grants an Interview

"And Pilate wondered if he were already dead; and summoning the centurion, he asked him whether he was already dead.

"And when he learned from the centurion that he was dead, he granted the body to Joseph.

"'Jesus of Nazareth?' says Pilate.

"'Yes.'

"'Dead already?'

"'Yes, sir.'

"'Crucified and died in what? Six hours?'

"'He was scourged first. He lost blood.'

"'So who doesn't get scourged? It still takes three days to die! And I saw this Jesus. A young man, intense and healthy, right? He was not weak. Clear-eyed, self-controlled, steadfast. Six hours?'

"'There was a storm, sir.'

"'I know. I live here.'

"'A strange storm. A really dreadful storm, sir.'

"'So, then! Exposure killed the King of the Jews! Or maybe Jupiter of Thunderbolts. So the others are dead too, right?'

"'No. They're alive.'

"'Right. And so is Jesus of Nazareth. No. You can't have his body. We're civilized. We bury the dead, sir, not the living. Get out.'

"'I promise you upon my honor that the man has died.'

"'You're a physician?'

"'No, sir.'

"'Then Jesus is sleeping. He's soporifer. Comatose, you understand? This Rabbi found a way to beat the pain—and you too, by the looks of it. Get out.'

"'Governor, I could prove his death, but there's so little time. It's almost sunset. I beg you to believe me. Jesus is dead. Dead and he must be buried. He can't be above when the sun goes down! Can I pay you? Can I buy the body, sir? I have money. What do you want? My rank? I'll give you my rank on the council. I give it away! Believe me— 'Shut up.'

"'—I touched his flesh, as cold as clay—'

"'Shut up! I'm tired of the business! I am tired of the day and the Jews and your thousand certitudes, your incomprehensible passions, wild-eyed, fanatic. You're all so... religious! Shut up, Joseph of Arimathea. Shut up. Get out.'

"'No.'

"'What?'

"'No. I can't leave. Not without his body. No.'

"'Raca! You idiot! Fatue! Do you know what I can do to you? Did you see what I did to your King?'

"'You killed him.'

"'I did not kill him! He is not dead! But I can kill you!'

"'It doesn't matter. I'm sorry, sir, but it really doesn't matter. Apart from him I am nothing anyway. I want to bury my Lord in dignity, with honor. Except for that, you can take whatever you want from me. Take my life!'

"'We are Romans! We do not bury the living!'

"'He is dead. There is no breath in his pale corpse. The blood is thickening in his extremities. He is dead.'

"'WHERE'S THAT CENTURION? BRING THE OFFICER IN CHARGE OF THE DAY'S EXECUTION. Now! You, Joseph, shut up. Wait and say nothing. I'll believe those paid to be honest. Besides, that old soldier's about to be pensioned, nothing to gain in a lie—and what do you think he thinks of your Jewish religious involutions? Right. We'll both defer to a pragmatist, a Roman—'

"And so there appears before the Governor a solid centurion: clear-eyed, controlled, immovable. Steadfast.

"'Yes, sir,' he says, 'Jesus of Nazareth is dead.'

"And then, without being asked, offering the thought of his own accord, he says, 'And you ought to release the body, sir, in order to bury him speedily. In dignity. With honor.'

"Pontius Pilate gapes at the centurion, then at Joseph. He stares back and forth from the fighter to the ruler, from the Roman to the Jew, from the hard man to the soft man, from the poor man to the rich—and he suffers a sort of disorientation because they look alike, these two. Brothers! All at once the supplicants look like brothers.

"Pilate is defeated.

"He believes this much: that Jesus is dead. He goes this far: o grant the corpse to Joseph.

"More than that... well, well, he's tired of the whole affair. He's sick to death of a people so completely, so unreasonably, so irredeemably religious!

"'Go on, get out. Both of you. Go.'

"They leave together.

* * *

"On Maundy Thursday, consider: we do bury the living, after all—and often! We bury the living Lord in the graves of ourselves whom he changes, by his indwelling, from tombs to living stones!

"This is the persistent gift of the Lord's last supper: that every time we faithfully eat and drink it, Jesus comes within us, and we become his temple here.

"JESUS:

"DEAD, YOU ENTERED JOSEPH'S TOMB
AND ONCE, FOR ALL, DID NOT EXIST.
ALIVE, YOU ENTER AND COMMUNE
MYSELF IN EVERY EUCHARIST.

"FOR THIS YOU MYSTIFIED THE WINE,
FOR THIS REDUCED THE BREAD TO BONE—
TO LODGE YOUR BODY, CHRIST, IN MINE!
THEN HERE, MY LOVE: COME HOME. COME HOME."

Walter Wangerin, Jr.
from Reliving the Passion (Zondervan, 1992), pp. 144-147

A Good Friday Meditation

"BEHOLD THE LAMB OF GOD WHO TAKES AWAY THE SIN OF THE WORLD and from His gracious look and gracious words, receive 'your mother' and 'your son' in your family and in your church.

"Look at Him too when He must go alone, even though our closest attention to Him cannot enter His terrible God-forsakenness. The depth of the abyss of hell and damnation, the wretched loss of God himself, is beyond our knowledge and experience. He alone goes to that far country. He has come from the secret heart of God. Now he opens up that secret.

"Angels sang at his birth. Angels came to serve him in the wilderness of temptation. Angels came to comfort him in his Gethsemanic sweat. But now there are no angels. Ten thousand times ten thousand of powerful and shining spirits, faces ablaze with indignation, swords drawn and singing, mounted on steeds chomping at the bit and pawing the sky for release, would have swooped to work a rescue that would have made the most powerful cavalry charge seem like a twitch of the nose. But God looks down on this Man of Sorrows, Grief, and Death, and says to the angels who love to do his will: "Stand back. Do not raise a finger to help. Verily, do not raise an eyelash."

"And God himself turned away.

"The burden is the burden of the Lamb atone.

"We are that terrible and lonely burden. He is the God who comes to us in our loneliness, forsakenness, and curse. Lost in the "non-place" of our aloneness, he comes to be our place. We cannot go to him. He comes to us. He is the Lamb of God who takes away the sins of the world. Caught in the enchantment of our self-love, bound in the enslavement of our own sin, strapped down by the Law's verdict of condemnation, and writhing in our shameful servitude, this Lamb comes to us. Well do we sing,

"'Blessed is he that cometh in the Name of the Lord! Hosanna-please save us.' Enough of this religious prattle that speaks of our doing this and deciding that. First he comes to us. He helps us, not by stepping on us, and not by shouting out commands for self-improvement at us, but by coming, by stooping down even under us to lift us up on his neck. lie humbled himself and became obedient unto death-even death by the cross. We are his burden.

"BEHOLD THE LAMB OF GOD WHO TAKES AWAY THE SIN OF THE WORLD.

"He isn't finished. You are not yet finished. But the work is finished: redemption is perfected and completed for you. The price has been paid, in full. Redemption by the Lamb has no missing pieces that you must fill in. It is perfected in order to perfect you. By his cross he has brought joy to the whole earth: he is out to perfect you in that joy. He who won the prize and paid the cost through suffering and death speaks the word of the perfected redemption to you so that you may know what you will be like when he is finished with you.

"Behold the Lamb of God who takes away the sin of the world. Adore him. Adore his cross. In him on that cross the perfection of heaven, with pure joy, is given to you. He was put to death that he might vivify his people.

"MERCIFUL JESUS, LAMB OF GOD, look on us that we may cling to you, and in your mercy have our peace forever."

Kenneth F. Korby

Karen Allison. April 1976

Easter

The Season of Easter

This is the season of excitement in the Church's year—and emotional turmoil in the life of a campus. Finally it's spring, and here in the Midwest that means variety: snow, sunshine, rain, wind, puddles, blue skies. Everything changes—usually every half hour. The light starts sooner and lasts longer, those grimy ice piles melt away, water runs down gutters, trees begin to green out, and little shoots of flowers poke up through dead leaves.

Along with these changes, school schedules fill up even tighter. Chapters that you haven't read yet now pile up, and paper deadlines don't seem so far away. There's pressure to get those last meetings in before the end of the year. Profs begin talking about review sessions before exams! You have to practice for juries, and scramble to fit in just one more concert. Things that seemed familiar now are speeded up, and life seems more full than we can manage. Is it possible that there's only a month or so left of this year that seemed so long back in September?

That's Easter, too. There's just more than you can take in. Sudden change is the key to the whole thing, as defeat becomes victory, death becomes life, sorrow becomes joy. This is the season where it is hardly possible to cram in all the joyous hymns that fill you with happiness. It's time to shake off the gloomy introspection of Lent and move into the full excitement of Christian hope and joy. This section reflects some of that sense of joy, of excitement, of thanksgiving for the blessings of this brief and beautiful season of Easter.

Celebrating Lives of Faith

(the following usually fall in the season of Easter)

March 31

John Donne (1631), priest and poet

BATTER MY HEART, THREE-PERSONED GOD; FOR YOU
AS YET BUT KNOCK, BREATHE, SHINE, AND SEEK TO MEND;
THAT I MAY RISE AND STAND, O'ERTHROW ME, AND BEND
YOUR FORCE TO BREAK, BLOW, BURN, AND MAKE ME NEW.
I, LIKE AN USURPED TOWN, TO ANOTHER DUE,
LABOR TO ADMIT YOU, BUT O, TO NO END;
REASON, YOUR VICEROY IN ME, ME SHOULD DEFEND,
BUT IS CAPTIVED, AND PROVES WEAK OR UNTRUE.
YET DEARLY I LOVE YOU, AND WOULD BE LOVED FAIN,
BUT AM BETROTHED UNTO YOUR ENEMY.
DIVORCE ME, UNTIE OR BREAK THAT KNOT AGAIN;
TAKE ME TO YOU, IMPRISON ME, FOR I,
EXCEPT YOU ENTHRALL ME, NEVER SHALL BE FREE,
NOR EVER CHASTE, EXCEPT YOU RAVISH ME.

April 6

Albrecht Durer (1528) and
Michaelangelo (1564), artists

"Lord, we give you thanks for those who teach us to see,
and in seeing the power to dream and seek and envision
the image that you would have us recognize as your own.
Seeing grace and seeing love come to us from the saints
and ministers whose works are images that nurture us.
Tarry not. We would see Jesus, your living Word of love.
In Christ's name we pray. Amen."

David Morgan

April 9
Dietrich Bonhoeffer, theologian and martyr

Few have ever understood the true cost of following You
Lord as did your faithful servant Dietrich Bonhoeffer. Look
with understanding and compassion upon me as I live in
the tension of my selfish desires and the desire to live as a
disciple devoted to you. Strengthen me, Lord Christ,
through your word, that I may not disappoint but ever
follow You with courage in spite of the cost. Amen.

April 23
Toyohiko Kagawa (1960), renewer of society

"Lord of all peoples, we thank You for those Your servants
who show us how to love You by loving those of Your
human family who are trampled and outcast, whoever and
wherever they are. We thank You for Your servant
Toyohiko, who showed the people of Japan the power of
Your love by serving the poor and downtrodden. Through
him you taught us all how active dedication to social
reform can change the moral climate of a whole society.
Help us likewise to serve You among the poor of our world
and so hold up the power of Your love for all to see and
marvel. Amen."

Theodore Ludwig

May 4
Monica (387), mother of Augustine

Mighty God, You have said that You are like a mother,
gathering little unsheltered creatures under Your
protecting wing. We thank You for the life and example of
Monica, whose faith and prayers helped Your Spirit to
bring Augustine to faith in You. Bless mothers as they pray
for their distracted, confused, and sometimes faithless
children, and grant that those prayers be as successful as
Monica's. Amen.

Special Days

The Resurrection of Our Lord

Collect from *LBW:* "O God, you gave your only Son to suffer death on the cross for our redemption, and by His glorious resurrection you delivered us from the power of death. Make us die every day to sin, so that we may live with Him forever in the joy of the resurrection; through Jesus Christ our Lord, who lives and reigns with you and the Holy Spirit, one God, now and forever. Amen."

reading: Luke 24:1-11. "Why do you look for the living among the dead?"

Meditation

We are accustomed to looking for the dead. Death pervades our existence. "Death and taxes," we claim, are the two things we can count on, and every politician (as least the ones who get elected) somewhere along the line promises to reduce taxes. No promises about death. Part of growing up is coming to terms with death. Hopefully it happens in little pieces at a time. Soon enough the big pieces of death come our way.

It comes as no surprise that much of life is in service to death, oriented towards death. We all cling to dying things and to some extent are in bondage to them. We take death for granted, death in all of the forms that it dogs our heels: poverty, war, crime, oppression, separation, betrayal—the list goes on and on, like tombstones in a graveyard. We make do with it, with life in the graveyard. Actually, it seems natural.

The women on Easter morning had no reason to be looking for anything other than death. Only the bright messengers in the tomb knew differently at that point.

Death was not the final word. Death did not possess the ultimate victory. Life was how things would end up, and death was counting its days.

So, get on with life. Shrug off the shrouds and say "NO" to the powers of death around you. The stone has been rolled away. Don't bring in an interior decorator to cozy up your tomb. Leave it!

Hymn Stanza

> THIS JOYFUL EASTERTIDE, AWAY WITH SIN AND SORROW!
> MY LOVE, THE CRUCIFIED, HAS SPRUNG TO LIFE THIS MORROW.
> HAD CHRIST, WHO ONCE WAS SLAIN, NOT BURST HIS THREE-DAY PRISON,
> OUR FAITH HAD BEEN IN VAIN. BUT NOW HAS CHRIST ARISEN, ARISEN, ARISEN;
> BUT NOW HAS CHRIST ARISEN!

Closing Prayer

God of empty tombs, coax me forth from my contentment with death. Grace me with the vision to recognize death and name it in every form that it takes. Empower me to settle for nothing less than life, even in that final moment when in darkness I wait upon Your ultimate, "Arise!" For Jesus' sake. Amen.

Ascension

Collect from *LBW*: "Almighty God, your only son was taken up into heaven and in power intercedes for us. May we also come into your presence and live forever in your glory; through your son, Jesus Christ our Lord, who lives and reigns with you and the Holy spirit, one God, now and forever. Amen."

reading: Luke 24: 44-53. "He opened their understanding, that they might understand the scriptures...."

Meditation

Now we have to do Christian life without Jesus, and sometimes that seems like the hardest job in the world. Certainly it must have been easier to know what Jesus would do when you could just ask Him? The disciples must have felt like actors when they first have to go "off book"—now there's nothing to lean on, we just have our own memory to carry us through. Looking up into the sky, it must have seemed very empty.

There are times when it seems very empty for all of us. We remember the excitement of festivals—the hush of Christmas Eve, the somber chanting on Maundy Thursday, the rush of joy at the Easter Vigil—but now? Now we have our understanding of the scriptures, which Jesus explained time after time, until His final explanation at the Last supper: "A new commandment I give you: that you love one another as I have loved you!" If that is the meaning of the scripture, then it could easily take a lifetime to understand and live it. At this moment, between Easter and Pentecost, that's the job we have been given, and we can start it any time.

Hymn Stanza

ALLELUIA! SING TO JESUS; HIS THE SCEPTER, HIS THE
THRONE; ALLELUIA! HIS THE TRIUMPH, HIS THE VICTORY
ALONE. HARK! THE SONGS OF PEACEFUL ZION THUNDER
LIKE A MIGHTY FLOOD:

"JESUS OUT OF EV'RY NATION HAS REDEEMED US BY
HIS BLOOD!"

ALLELUIA! NOT AS ORPHANS ARE WE LEFT IN
SORROW NOW;
ALLELUIA! HE IS NEAR US, FAITH BELIEVES, NOR
QUESTIONS HOW.
THOUGH THE CLOUD FROM SIGHT RECEIVED HIM WHEN
THE FORTY DAYS WERE O'ER,
SHALL OUR HEARTS FORGET HIS PROMISE "I AM WITH
YOU EVERMORE""

(LBW #158)

Closing Prayer

Let us not forget, Lord Jesus Christ, that though we do not
see You in our midst as You appeared long ago, we must
learn to see You now in our neighbor, in each other, and
in ourselves. Continue to speak for us at the throne of the
Almighty God, and bring us finally into union with You in
those heavenly mansions of which You spoke. Amen.

Prayers of the Season

For those who love to celebrate Easter at the Chapel of the Resurrection

Lord, I love your house, and I am glad for the chance to spend this solemn and holy season here in this awesome Chapel. Help me to be the kind of Christian whose church-going is a helpful example to others, to be devout without being judgmental. Let my piety be warm and loving, knowing that others love You in their own ways. Thank You for the efforts and talents of those who work at worship here, spending long hours in practice and study to make these marvelous occasions. Bless us all as we remember the greatness of Your sacrifice, and the majesty of Your triumph over death. Give me the will to bring news of this greatness and majesty to others in ways that are meaningfully real—by feeding the hungry and caring for the needy and sick. Without this expression of love in action, all my joy in Your glory is hollow and pointless. Help me to grow in loving both worship and service for Your sake. Amen.

For those who celebrate Easter missing home

Dear Lord, I know that the meaning of the season is the same whether I'm at home or away, and yet I really miss my home and family and the way we do things there. I want to experience the joy of Your resurrection, but I feel sad that there's just a Dining Service Easter Dinner—I know the staff tried, but I almost cried when I thought of the table at home. Please help me to feel the presence that really counts, and to know that in doing my work here I am following You toward the joy that matters. Amen.

For strength as a musician in the Church

I hope You know, God, how much work this season is for a musician! Every time I turn around, somebody wants another accompaniment, another choir setting, another rehearsal or performance. Do You think it would be possible sometime to have an Easter celebration in silence? OK, I'm joking, but I'm tired! Give me strength to get through it with more than merely grim existence. Thank You for my talents, and help me to use them while at the same time knowing the joys of the season like those who aren't working so hard at it. Amen.

For Easter hope in times of sorrow

Lord God, the promise of resurrection comes to me hard right now, since I am feeling sorrow and loss. Keep me connected to Your promise, so that as my feelings waver and change, I trust Your faithfulness. Let me be aware of others' joy without envy. Hold me with Your powerful and loving hand. For the sake of Jesus. Amen.

For those who do not believe

I want to come before You in this moment, Lord, on behalf of my friend who sees nothing in the story of Your resurrection but misguided superstition. Nothing I can say seems to affect this conviction, and I'm at the point where I know that overcoming this disbelief will take a gift of Your Spirit. Please send it to the heart of my friend, and lift him/her up into belief. In your name. Amen.

In thanks for the goodness of God's creation

This day has been so wonderfully beautiful that I have to come into Your presence to thank You as Creator. Each little change is such a special miracle, and the freshness of air and sky so restorative! I am aware as I look and smell and feel the world around me that You, too, love the earth and all its creatures and weathers. Thank You for the beauty and goodness of this creation, now rising again out of winter sleep. Amen.

Spring weekend

It's the last fling of the year, Lord, then I'll really get serious and hit the books. Promise. Everyone else will be doing that, too, and that will help. But really, these years are about more than classes, right? So, Lord, let this weekend be a good and fun and safe mix with friends. Equip us more fully to be for each other what You would have us be. And refresh us for studies ahead. Amen.

In thanks for insights

Yesterday was what we call a beautiful day, and today—ugh! rainy, gray skies and cold, bitter wind. Everybody's complaining about it, but I did have an insight as I was crossing the tundra—I suddenly knew that the cold and rain are part of the whole cycle, part of what is necessary to make the green and blossoming days we enjoy. So, thanks for the insight, and thanks even for the stormy rains! Amen.

Uncertainty about returning

Only you, Lord, could know how lonely I feel right now, with everybody else talking about next year, and my own plans so uncertain. There is so much I don't understand about my life, and my future, and it seems so much harder when all around me there is this constant chatter that seems so sure of itself. Help me to work through these problems, help me to get hold of the fear that paralyzes me. Give me a calm and cheerful spirit, so that whatever happens, I know that You are with me. Amen.

At the ending of a school year

I think my emotions never have been as mixed as they are right now, Lord, as I face the end of this year. When I think through all that I have learned, I'm proud—and even a little amazed. When I think about what will change now, about the friends who will not be back next year, I'm sad—and even a little afraid. Bless us all as we go on to our hometowns and summer jobs, and make the time pass quickly, so that we can get back to our lives together here. Amen.

A teacher's prayer at Commencement

Now is the right time, Lord, to remember that "goodbye" is short for "God be with you." Some of these graduates are the best students I've ever taught, and I've come to love them. They give me such a tremendous sense of gratitude that I've been able to be with them, and a great humility in the face of their talent. Stay with them, keep them from cynicism and false pride. Let their ideals move them to great service and greater achievement. I pray, most of all, that what I have taught will be a benefit in whatever lies ahead for them. Amen.

A graduating senior's prayer

Lord God, you know by now my feelings of excitment and anxiety; I don't have to go through them again at this moment. But in this frenzy of winding things up, let me be truly aware of all that I want to remember and treasure. Help me to notice and store up all the little things that I will miss, and give me a true appreciation of all the great things that have been part of my life here. Give me the patience and selflessness to thank everybody who has helped me. Make Commencement—the day that I have dreamed of for so long—be a perfect day for me and all those I love. Amen.

Arbor Day (last Friday of April)

"Gracious God, thank you for cedars, elms, pines, redwoods, maples, weeping willows—all the wonderful trees that flourish around us. Emerging within the life patterns of this planet, we give you thanks for them all, for we love them dearly. Upon the wood of a tree You gave Yourself for us as well, in a manner beyond our comprehension, yet we stretch our limbs and soar with the grace and love poured out upon us there. Stir us up to cherish and preserve the trees You have given—essential to our life and signs of Your gracious love. Amen."

David H. Kehret

From the Chapel

Our New Song
Easter 2, 1982

> "'SO LET US KEEP THE FESTIVAL
> TO WHICH THE LORD INVITES US;
> CHRIST IS HIMSELF THE JOY OF ALL,
> THE SUN THAT WARMS AND LIGHTS US.
> NOW HIS GRACE TO US IMPARTS
> ETERNAL SUNSHINE TO OUR HEARTS
> THE NIGHT OF SIN IS ENDED.'

"We dare to sing a song. And it is not simply a dirge of lament nor a cry for love and satisfaction. It is a song of celebration. We eat and drink not simply to feed ourselves but to celebrate the life which is ours. It is a most daring thing to do. Who dares to sing a song in a world where thousands starve each day? Who dares to sing when nations war against nations? Who dares to sing when many suffer from unemployment, from anxiety and worry? Who dares to sing when friends and loved ones suffer sickness and grief? Some people might sing a song to escape from all that, to close their eyes and for a moment forget it all. But that is not the song of Easter. This song springs from the soul of those who have looked yet deeper. In his most recent novel, the South African writer Alan Paton speaks of his beautiful land. Alan Paton has struggled all his life against the unjust apartheid that afflicts his country. He has never closed his eyes to injustice or refused the suffering that conies with his struggle. Yet, in the midst of this he can still see deeper and sing his song.

"This faith took Thomas and the disciples out of their locked room into the world. They went, as they were sent, to do the work of Christ. And Easter has to penetrate into our locked rooms. There are times when we feel very much alone. Friends whom we trusted fail us; they even hurt us. We lock the doors of our hearts with resentment. 153

"'If that's the way they want to treat me, I'll go my own way.' Christ comes to give us peace. And he sends us back once again. Or there are times we feel threatened by the world of the university. We are bombarded with new ideas and new facts. We cannot fit all this into the patterns of our past life and our old ways of thinking. We bolt the doors of our minds against what threatens, we draw the shades which would let this painful light into our lives. We turn to our Lord for peace. And he sends us out again into that world, He sends us back to the endless stream of questions where every answer only provokes a new question. But now we can see light and life."

Dale Lasky

Sing Joy!

Isaiah 61:1-4

"'Ho everyone who thirsts, come to the waters; and he who has no money, come buy and eat.'

"Ho everyone: Listen to Isaiah shouting! At least this once we ought to join him; get chins out of our hands; unglue ourselves from chairs and pews. At least this once we ought to shout and sing and look alive! The Word has gone out. The invitation has arrived.

"'Invitation for what? What are we celebrating?' He was called Jesus, Son of God, Savior. We can't afford to miss this celebration, not when this kind of food and drink is being served. We can't waste time primping before the mirror, trying to cover our pock-marked skins with powder and paint; trying to hide our deformed bodies with velvet and fur. Come! Come as we are! The Word has gone out. Today we are acceptable. No tally sheets, no statistics, no dressing up or down, no skills, no talents, no money, no work, no hymns, no prayers—nothing—will make us more acceptable than we are right now. We are honored guests. We are wanted at the table—no matter where we were before, or how we looked, or what we said—no matter now. The Son, the Father's only Son, washes our hands and feet and gives us new clothes, he introduces us to the Father, and the Father, stretching out his hand, makes room for us at the table.

"Eat, drink, and be merry for today and tomorrow and tomorrow we are alive!

"Lord, have mercy on us.

"We are so often hard-of-hearing: accepting Your invitation but only on our terms; hearing the Word about receiving Your Life but missing the part about giving up our own. We are so often distracted listeners: attending the celebration but only on our terms; wanting to be seated at the Father's table but confusing this with instant happiness. We are so often completely deaf: writing our own invitations, organizing our own celebrations, talking a great deal and hearing nothing.

"Christ have mercy on us.

"Do not leave us alone listening to ourselves. Shout the lively Word into our ears so that in spite of our deficient hearing we will listen. Shout Your forgiveness at us with vigor that indeed Your Word will go in both ears and never stop coming out our mouths; so that we may be the constant stream of Your Word—healing, forgiving, bringing new Life to each one who hears us speak.

"Lord have mercy on us.

"We are so often tongue-tied: having heard the forgiving Word we are reluctant to make it public; we retreat into mumbling. We so often try to improvise: we add and sub-tract from the clear forgiving Word to suit the occasion and our own convenience. We are so often completely dumb: our tongues are paralyzed with fear— fear of giving away, of losing, some part of our life—and so the clear forgiving Word is not spoken.

"Christ have mercy on us.

"Do not leave us alone talking to ourselves. Loosen our vocal chords and our tongues so that in spite of our de-fective speech we can make Your Word intelligible. Place the clear Word on the tips of our tongues so that when we speak we have something to say. Make us so sure of Your Life that we can forget about ours and we can be the constant stream of Your healing forgiving Word.

"Lord have mercy.

"Christ have mercy.

"Lord have mercy.

"'The Lord has anointed Me and I anoint you. The Father has sent Me and I send you. I am not there now to touch and speak and smile and cry, but you are, and My Spirit is in you. I am not there now to bless the bread and divide the fish, to gather the children, to bandage the wounded, to walk with the stumblers, to sit with the scorned, to die between thieves—but you are, and My Spirit is in you. You have been gathered and brought to the Father. My Spirit, My own breath, is keeping you alive. It is time for you to be scattered and sent away—to suffer, to mourn, to die for My other children—and so will you live! You have no more to do with death. You have Life. You are now sent to grasp, to clench, to smother, to choke. You are sent to give, to open, to unlock, to touch, to speak, to smile, to cry.

"'Do not misunderstand or obscure My words with convenient explanations. To feed the hungry means to give away your plate of meat and potatoes. To clothe the naked means to give away your shoes and overcoat. To give a drink to the thirsty means to give away your last cup of water. To die means to give away even your self-respect. There must be nothing between us. There must be nothing in your hands but My hands. The world expects some contribution, some payment, some work by which your life can be recognized. Bring none of these to Me. Come with empty hands. Come with hands wide and fingers spread apart. You are given one day at a time, not to be scrimped and shriveled and hidden and saved—one day at a time—to be given, offered, spent until there is nothing left.'

"'Joy and fear do not live in the same house. With joy the Father sets His table for us. With joy He brings us to His house. With joy He calls us sons. Sing joy! Sing Joy! The Son, the Word of the Father, has lived with us, still lives with us. Walk out into the streets and tell the people. Show them how He did it: Break the loaf of bread and give it to the hungry ones who stand along the curb-ing. Pour a cold drink of water for the thirsty ones who watch from balconies and windows. Run after the fright-ened ones who crouch in darkened doorways. Shake hands with the lonely ones who have been pushed to the edge of the crowd. Put an arm around the crippled ones who need to lean on someone.

"Touch. Speak. Smile. Cry.

"Do not be afraid. We are doing it for Him. We have His Name. We have His Word.

"We have His Promise. We have His Joy. How can we keep quiet?

"Eat, drink, and be merry for today and tomorrow and tomorrow we are alive!"

Anne Zink Springsteen
excerpted from The Cresset, December 1967, pp. 8-9

Seeing the Christ

Easter 3, 1980

John 21:1-14

"How does this Christ appear to us? I dare say that most of us have not seen Jesus with these sense organs. Nor, I suspect, have many of us seen him in a dramatic flash of light, or even heard his voice like Paul did. Yet the Church has always claimed to see him and to know his presence with the eyes of faith. By the Holy Spirit's power, he is known to be present in the baptismal waters that join us to his cross and resurrection. He appears to the faithful in the breaking of bread at this table; in bread and wine and the words 'for you,' he makes his presence known. It is his voice we hear when we grasp those precious words, 'In the name and in the stead of our Lord Jesus Christ, I forgive you all your sins.' He even appears to us in the persons of our brothers and sisters who, with us, make up his own body. He appears to us in the needy one who needs my listening, my caring, my prayers. He appears to us in the brother or sister who comes into our neediness; to care about us, to share our sorrow, confusion and joy, to encourage us on our way, to bear us up with a smile and a touch. So it is that the risen Christ appears to us today.

"It seems to me that his appearance is often quite unexpected too, like it was for those seven fishermen. The big Jesus event was over now, it seemed. He'd done his things—even died and rose again. But the excitement had all died down and it was time to get back to the normal routines of fishing for a living. Sounds a lot like us, who were carried so high on waves of Easter excitement just two weeks ago. Since then, well, it's back to reality; back to the old grind; back to the usual work and play. Judging from the empty seats last Sunday and again today, we might even suspect that the crowd has lapsed into a kind of post-Easter indifference, maybe even living as though it hadn't really happened; or, if it did, maybe it doesn't really matter.

"Jesus interrupted the fishermen. He broke into their business-as-usual routines and called them to remember his living and giving presence. Jesus interrupted Paul's business too, that awful business of trying to stop the Jesus story dead in its tracks. Jesus intervened and turned things around. So with us, too, Jesus comes into the ordinariness of our lives; calling us to rise up out of our post-Easter indifference, calling us out of our daily opposition to him, calling us out of our preoccupation with fun and games and with those frightful deadlines, calling us to see and trust his presence again. Yes, my friends, it is in the ordinariness of preaching, baptizing, communing at his altar; it is in the ordinariness of daily routines and even in our opposition to him that the risen Christ appears to us. Pray that we might have the eyes to see him.

"And what happens when the risen Christ appears? People's lives are turned around. For the fishing crew it meant, 'Feed my lambs, feed my sheep, feed my lambs.' They were sent with a task to do. Their lives would never be the same. They were sent to tell the story by their words, their lives and their deaths. So, too, with Paul; his call from the risen Christ was not only a call to be healed and to become a reconciled friend of God; it was also a call to go and testify to the victory of the cross of Jesus. In word and deed Paul went out into the world determined to know nothing but Christ the crucified and to tell of the new life that was offered by that crucified one. When the risen Christ appears to people, he sends them on a mission; he sends us out to tell.

"Finally, when Christ appears to us, we are drawn into the song of the heavenly liturgy, which we hear in the reading from the Revelation of St. John. We are drawn into the great company of the elders, the myriads of angels and all the hosts of God's saints from every time and every place; we join their heavenly song:

"'Worthy is the Lamb who was slain, to receive power and wealth and wisdom and might and honor and glory and blessing.' When Christ appears to us we cannot but worship and adore him.

"So today, as every day, we come before him with empty nets. The risen Christ is here to fill them with his every saving gift. And when our nets are filled, he sends us out to share those gifts wherever we go. As we go we sing the praises of the Lamb who was slain. Come now and eat with him that you may be filled with his very special joy and precious new life.

"In the name of the Father and of the Son and of the Holy Spirit. Amen."

Edgar P. Senne

The spring commencement ceremonies come most years near the end of the Easter season. Those events always include the assembly's singing of Valparaiso University's Alma Mater.

HAIL TO THE BROWN AND GOLD!
WE PLEDGE THEE TO UPHOLD
WHEREVER WE MAY BE
THY HONORED NAME.
THROUGH YEARS THAT COME AND GO,
TO PAY THE DEBT WE OWE
WE'LL E'ER BE TRUE TO YOU,
DEAR OLD VALPO.

HAIL TO THE BROWN AND GOLD!
RECALL THE DAYS OF OLD,
THE HAPPY DAYS WHICH WE
NE'ER SHALL FORGET.
AS SHADOWS LONGER GROW
BRIGHTER THE FLAME SHALL GLOW,
THE FLAME OF LOVE FOR YOU,
DEAR OLD VALPO.

HAIL TO THE BROWN AND GOLD!
THEY SONS AND DAUGHTERS HOLD
IN LOVING LOYALTY
THY COLORS DEAR;
COLORS WHEREBY THEY SHOW
WHAT OTHERS, TOO, SHOULD KNOW;
THAT THEY BELONG TO YOU,
DEAR OLD VALPO.

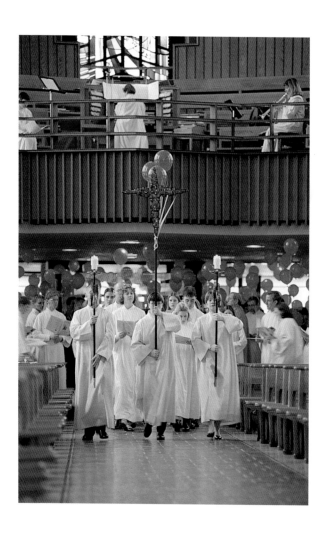

Ye also shall bear
witness ... because
they have not
known the father
nor me.

Suzanne Kayser. May 1964

Pentecost

The Season of Pentecost

Like most seasons of the church year, Pentecost begins
with a festival, but unlike others, it then goes on and on
for as many as 27 possible weeks! Pentecost Sunday comes
50 days after Easter, and commemorates the day when
Jesus' disciples received the gift of the Holy Spirit. In some
ways, it seems to say, "OK, the big excitements of
Christmas and Easter and Ascension are past; now it's time
to get on with living the Christian life." That may be why,
in some quarters, these Sundays are numbered as the
Sundays in ordinary time.

And Pentecost is the season when most of us scatter across
the country, out of school, back to hometowns and
summer jobs and family ties. The campus looks
different—parking lots empty, groups of campers or
cheerleaders or Elderhostelers wander around, paint crews
appear out of nowhere. The frantic pace of school year
schedule gives way to another rhythm. Those on campus
work at longer-term projects, getting back to the book
manuscript, or imagining a new development that requires
research and grant writing, for instance. And all over the
country, where students have scattered, people are living
their everyday lives—lives in ordinary time.

This is the season where we live out the implications of
the dramatic Christian story we've just been through during
the rest of the year. This is where the Christ we've waited
for in Advent gives us direction for a world waiting for
justice and peace. This is where the infant Jesus of
Christmas softens our hearts and makes us gentle. This is
where the baptized Christ of Epiphany leads us through
repentance every day to new expectations. And this is

where, because of the Jesus crucified and risen, we live by
grace-filled hope in a world that too readily encourages
despair or oblivion. These are the days of ordinary time,
made extraordinary by our discipleship with this Jesus.

That is why, in this prayer book, we've gathered here a
collection of prayers for the many occasions of ordinary
life. There are prayers of thanksgiving and joy, as well as
prayers of petition, sorrow, and repentance. Formally, the
season of Pentecost lasts all the way till the next Advent
begins, but in these pages, it will stand for that long
segment of the year where we show what we're made of,
Christians living in ordinary time.

Celebrating Lives of Faith

(the following usually fall in the season of Pentecost)

June 11

St. Barnabas, Apostle

Grant, O God that I may learn from the example of Your faithful servant Barnabas, who gave so generously for the relief of the poor. In dedicating his life to You he did not seek public acknowledgement but only the well-being of Your Church. Open my heart to give of myself generously that I may know the joy of serving You, Jesus Christ my Lord. Amen.

June 29

St. Peter and St. Paul

"Almighty God, whose blessed apostles Peter and Paul glorified you by their martyrdom: Grant that Your Church, instructed by their teaching and example, and knit together in unity by Your Spirit, may ever stand firm upon the one foundation, which is Jesus Christ our Lord. Amen."

(prayer from LBW)

July 22

St. Mary Magdalene

Your servant Mary Magdalene was a searcher, Lord Jesus. You were the one she sought outwardly to find, and You taught her to inwardly keep searching for the truth of Your resurrection and love. Teach me as well, gracious Lord, so that I, too, may boldly give witness to the power of the resurrection and the life You freely give. Amen.

July 28
Johann Sebastian Bach and George Frederick Handel, musicians of the Church

God of splendor and majesty, You equipped Your servants Bach and Handel to passionately proclaim the story of salvation through powerful works of music. I thank You for these evangelists of word and song whose work remains unmatched in its beauty. Continue to use their creative legacy to inspire and revive my soul with the song of Your unending love in Christ Jesus my Lord. Amen.

August 15
Mary, Mother of our Lord

In your wisdom, Lord, you chose Mary to be the vessel by which your Son would become fully human. Obediently she embraced the purpose for which You called her, only to have her heart pierced with grief as she stood as a sentinel of love at the foot of His cross. Thank you for Mary's mothering love that nurtured the love He sacrificed for the sins of the whole world, Jesus Christ my Lord. Amen.

August 28
St. Augustine

Merciful and patient God, today I remember one whose struggles in life were not unlike my own. I wrestle with doubt and often wonder what my purpose is in this life. Help me discern Your purpose for me, as You did so patiently for Your servant Augustine. Turn me away from the empty desires of my flesh that fail to satisfy and grant me a light of serenity to flood my heart that all darkness of doubt may vanish away, through Jesus Christ our Lord I pray. Amen.

Special Days

Pentecost

Prayer of the Day from *LBW:* "God, the Father of our Lord Jesus Christ, as you sent upon the disciples the promised gift of the Holy Spirit, look upon your Church and open our hearts to the power of the Spirit. Kindle in us the fire of your love, and strengthen our lives for service in your kingdom; through your Son, Jesus Christ our Lord, who lives and reigns with you in the unity of the Holy Spirit, one God, now and forever. Amen."

reading: John 20:20-23 "...receive the Holy Spirit...."

Meditation

Pentecost may have caused more problems than we realize. At Pentecost the presence of the Holy Spirit creates a gifted people. With the giving of gifts comes also the power to forgive sins for where there is an abundance of gifts there is a need to be ready to forgive. You see, gifts tend to make us jealous, defensive, and even aggressive. Therefore we need the peace Christ came to bring, the power to forgive and patience to endure. Pentecost creates a Church of exceptionally gifted people with hopes, talents, and strengths that are unbeatable. Whatever the challenges we may face as a people of God, with regard to the use or misuse of the gifts we have, it is a relief to know that we can turn to the wounded Jesus on the cross. It is in Christ that we find unity and power to forgive.

Hymn Stanzas

CREATOR SPIRIT, HEAV'NLY DOVE,
DESCEND UPON US FROM ABOVE;
WITH GRACES MANIFOLD RESTORE
YOUR CREATURES AS THEY WERE BEFORE

TO YOU, THE COMFORTER, WE CRY,
TO YOU THE GIFT OF GOD MOST HIGH,
TRUE FOUNT OF LIFE, THE FIRE OF LOVE,
THE SOUL'S ANOINTING FROM ABOVE.

Closing Prayer

Come, Holy Spirit! Come and be my sweet refreshment, my
solace and peace, my light in darkness. Heal my wounds,
water my dryness and warm my sometimes—cold heart.
Bring me into the safety of the home you provide that I
may know the joy of sharing my gifts with my family and
the Church. In Christ's name I pray. Amen.

Holy Trinity

Prayer of the Day from *LW:* "Almighty and everlasting God, since you have given us, your servants, grace to acknowledge the glory of the eternal Trinity by the confession of a true faith, and to worship the true Unity in the power of your divine majesty, keep us also steadfast in this true faith and worship, and defend us ever from all our adversaries; for you, O Father, Son, and Holy Spirit, live and reign, one God, now and forever. Amen."

reading: Matthew 28:16-20 " ...I am with you always to the end of the age."

Meditation

One of the oldest icons of the Trinity is entitled "Hospitality of Abraham." It depicts Abraham and Sara serving the three visitors who announced that Sarah would bear a son in her old age. Early church fathers believed this to be an early revelation of the Trinity.

The angels on the icon appear in perfect harmony and oneness yet each is unique. Rather than seen in a hierarchical order the Trinity is shown as a circle of love extended to the world. Such is the nature of the God, Father, Son and, Holy Spirit. God is love. The day we set aside to reflect on the mystery of the Holy Trinity is less about a doctrinal formulation and more about the intertwining purposes of God revealed in each person of the Trinity. This revelation is celebrated today as we rejoice in the creative, redeeming, and sanctifying work of God continued in us and through us with power and love.

Hymn Stanza

TRIUNE GOD, OH, BE OUR STAY; OH, LET US PERISH
NEVER!
CLEANSE US FROM OUR SINS, WE PRAY, AND GRANT US
LIFE FOREVER.
KEEP US FROM THE EVIL ONE; UPHOLD OUR FAITH MOST
HOLY,
AND LET US TRUST YOU SOLELY WITH HUMBLE HEARTS
AND LOWLY.
LET US PUT GOD'S ARMOR ON, WITH ALL TRUE
CHRISTIANS RUNNING.
OUR HEAVN'LY RACE AND SHUNNING THE DEVIL'S WILES
AND CUNNING.
AMEN, AMEN! THIS BE DONE; SO SING WE, "ALLELUIA!"

LW #170

Closing Prayer

Triune God, Holy Three, preserve me in your love and
reveal through me the love you have for all the world.
Give to me unquestioned commitment to your purposes as
you use me to serve those who are lonely, distressed,
hurting, and unloved. Give me faith to know the mystery
of your presence and may the word of good news be
always on my lips, a living liturgy of praise to the glory of
you, Father, Son, and Holy Spirit. Amen.

Prayers of the Season

Summer job

Ok, God, I'm on my way to work, first day of my summer job. You have opened a door for me, and I'm walking through. There must be something here You want me to do. Help me do it. There must be something here You want me to learn. Open me to it. There must be some way You want me to be your hand reaching into this place. Lead me to see it. For Jesus' sake. Amen.

Living at home

No, they didn't move my bed out to the garage, Lord, or turn my room into a den. But it's an adjustment living at home again. For all of us. Help my parents trust me to handle my own affairs at home as much as they presume I do at school. And remind me that living in a family rather than in a residence hall, I also owe them consideration and a helping hand—and possibly a word as to when I expect to get home. Amen.

Reconnecting with home church

What a mixture of feelings, God, back worshiping in my home congregation. I have a history here. Now I feel like a visitor, even a prodigal. I've been away and worshiped in other ways. My world has expanded and shifted since I sat in these pews. Help me be who I've become, making that a gift, and help me receive people here as the gifts they'll always be to me. Amen.

Feeling cut off from friends

Thank you, God, for email. Amen.

From the Chapel

In this final season of the church year, "From the Chapel" contains excerpts of 7 thought-provoking messages. Each poses, and addresses, a question that students, faculty, and staff have pondered over the years.

What Do We Dream?

Acts 2:17-18

"Few words have greater breadth or depth of meaning for us than the word 'dream.' Popular ballads of my youth advised, 'Dream when you're feeling blue; dream, that's the thing to do.' The Everly Brothers consoled us, 'Whenever I want you, all I have to do is dream.' In the movie, 'Field of Dreams,' an Iowa farmer heard a voice assuring him that if he built a baseball diamond in his cornfield, 'they will come.'

"Our experiences have taught us that dreams can stimulate our vision and spur progress, or dreams can seduce us away from pursuing useful tasks and can lead to personal disintegration. Dreams may give us insights into ourselves, for they may reveal our deepest thoughts and emotions; but we all know that following one's dreams to their logical conclusions does not always produce the gratification for which we hoped.

"The ceremonies of this day and the diplomas you will receive this afternoon suggest that at least some of your dreams have come true. I am guessing that as you reflect on those dreams, you realize that some have been exceeded and some did not turn out the way you dreamed. As VU graduates, you carry within yourselves the knowledge, skills and attitudes to pursue and achieve the American dream. At the same time, the critical and analytical skills you have learned may cause you to wonder what you really accomplish if you succeed.

"Whatever your thoughts and feelings this morning, you may identify with the words of the Apostle Peter as he quoted the Prophet Joel. 'In the last days, God declares, I will pour out my spirit on all flesh, and your sons and your daughters shall prophesy, and your young men shall see visions, and your old men shall dream dreams. Even upon my slaves, both men and women, in those days I will pour out my spirit and they shall prophesy.'

"For Peter and the other disciples, Pentecost meant a dream come true, but in a much different form than they first imagined. They had been on an emotional roller coaster for three years. They had been lifted to glorious expectations when their dreams seemed limitless. At other times their most cherished dreams had been dashed.

"Today, you see your dream becoming reality. If you are honest, you will admit that your dream has been reshaped during your years on this campus. Like the disciples of Jesus, your experiences at Valparaiso University may have been an emotional roller coaster—glorious expectations that seemed limitless, experiences that almost crushed the dream, then back to the mountain top of optimism. Here your experiences parallel those of Peter and the others at Pentecost. All we have described thus far are personal dreams—Peter's dreams, your dreams, human dreams. At the heart of Pentecost is God's dream for the church, for human beings, for you!

"God has a dream for you, and during your years on this campus, that dream has been recounted over and over in a variety of settings. Each year at VU, the entire dream of God has been shared with you. The Scripture lessons read during the Eucharist services and Morning Prayer, in theology classes or bible study groups, have conveyed aspects of God's dream for humankind to you. Our confession of faith in the Apostles' and Nicene Creeds, the silent witness of the stained glass windows of this chapel, the towering figure of the Christus Rex, all convey components of God's dream that culminates in our salvation. All those words, symbols, and memories will assist you to reflect again and again upon God's dream for all of us as you leave this place.

"Christ's sending His Spirit instituted a new era in the lives of His followers. The Holy Spirit enabled the disciples to implement the components of God's dream. The Spirit's presence gave God's dream new clarity and urgency. The dream was all about Jesus and how His life, His death, and His resurrection give meaning to the assertion that God loves His people.

"As God's dream comes to greater fulfillment on Pentecost, that fulfillment testifies to the dream's power. God's dream is not like the foggy mist that sometimes descends on Valparaiso, for that mist eventually lifts and is forgotten like many of our dreams. God's dream is given substance by the person of the Holy Spirit.

"While VU is not a church but a university, many here are members of the community of faith called together by God's Spirit. All who are part of this spiritual community called by the Holy Spirit, nurtured through the Word and the sacraments, and strengthened in faith by the witness of God's people, carry in our persons the wherewithal to share God's dream with other people.

"In our best moments, we Christians dream of the day when people from all nations, ethnic backgrounds, and racial groups will come together in worship of Jesus as Lord and Savior of the world. Christian people take seriously the responsibility to help make this happen. Because of that, some accuse us of being too aggressive, too pushy, too evangelistic. History shows that we can be deterred from our God-given, Spirit-motivated activism, but when we succumb to that pressure, we forget what we are all about. We are dreamers called to share God's dream with others so they can become dreamers as well.

"As you leave this campus I encourage you to dream. Continue to dream your own personal dreams, but do so in the spirit of Pentecost, mindful of God's dream for you. The dream of God, once viewed as impossible, is a magnificent dream filled with hope and positive expectation. Because of God's dream and the ministry of God's Spirit, you can leave this place today empowered and prepared to share God's magnificent dream with others."

Alan F. Harre
homily at Baccalaureate Service, May 18, 1997

What Do We Proclaim?

Acts 2:1-13

"Nothing like it had ever happened before. Nothing like it is likely ever to happen again.

"But Pentecost is a miracle which, in a less dramatic way, the Spirit of God performs every day. For while any man can learn another language if he is willing to give sufficient time and effort to it, no man can call Jesus Lord but by the Holy Ghost. Therefore every time we call Jesus Lord we speak a language which is not native to us. We speak, in sober fact, as the Spirit gives us utterance.

"And when we speak thus, chances are that we will get the same reaction that Peter and the apostles got from many in the crowd on that first Pentecost. 'You're full of new wine,' 'You're crazy,' 'I don't dig you,' 'What kind of preacher talk is that?'—these are all ways of expressing the same reaction, a reaction of unbelief and sometimes hostility to the Gospel. And this need not surprise us, for the Gospel really is foolishness to those who do not believe.

"But not everyone will mock us as madmen or drunks. Through the Word spoken by His people God adds to the church those who should be saved. There is a power in the Gospel which gives a kind of eloquence even to our fumbling and stumbling speech—not perhaps the eloquence of a Peter or a Paul but the simple eloquence of a child describing his father, of a shipwrecked sailor telling how he was rescued.

"Pentecost was a miracle. But wherever the Holy Spirit is present in the Word, miracles happen. For faith itself is a great miracle, and every Christian is a living testimony to the miraculous working of the Holy Spirit."

John Strietelmeier,
Off-Key Phrases (St. Louis: Concordia, 1968), pp. 58-59.

Who Do We Listen To?

"If He calls you, you shall say, 'Speak, Lord; for Thy servant hears.'"

1 Samuel 3:9

"In today's text, old Eli, the priest, gives advice to young Samuel which can provide a clue for making the learning experience here at Valparaiso University more worthwhile. Samuel thought he heard the Lord calling in the night. Eli told him to listen with his heart and respond with the words, 'Speak, Lord, for Thy servant heareth.'

"Samuel had been dedicated by his mother as a young child to service in the tabernacle. There he learned much from the priests and attendants. He must have been an able student, for the account says he 'grew on and was in favor both with the Lord and also with men.'

"The expression 'he grew on' pretty well sums up the idea of education. It is a growth process. A university is in the business of encouraging growth. Books, classes, and teachers provide keys that unlock great storehouses of knowledge. Growth has to do with how we respond to opportunities for learning. There is a calling to be a student or teacher, just as there is to be a nurse, or a pastor, or anything else.

"How do you measure growth of this kind? Obviously the lengthening transcript of grades and credits does not tell the whole story. It has to be described in terms of the development of personality, and the sharpening of mental and spiritual insights. If your learning in this place nudges you in the direction of becoming a well-rounded person with a disciplined mind, capable of thoughtful reflection, then we are achieving at least a part of our goal.

"'Speak, Lord, for Thy servant heareth.' You have to have a listening heart to take advantage of any education. You have to open yourself to the marvels of God's creation, nurture the spark of curiosity, and sense the excitement of the chase in the search for ideas. Many an apple fell from the tree before Isaac Newton watched one fall and from it derived a whole new concept about the motions of the universe.

"We are all tempted just to go through forms and routines day after day and hope for the best. But I would like to believe that here we remind you often enough of the implications of Elizabeth Barrett Browning's lines:

> "'EARTH'S CRAMMED WITH HEAVEN,
>   AND EVERY COMMON BUSH AFIRE WITH GOD,
>   AND ONLY HE WHO SEES TAKES OFF HIS SHOES—
>   THE REST SIT ROUND IT AND PLUCK BLACKBERRIES.'

"'Speak, Lord.' We need God's voice. Not that there isn't a cacophony of voices already. In Samuel's day all sorts of spokesmen invited allegiance to false gods. It was hard to hear the Lord in the midst of claims and counterclaims. Samuel had to listen pretty carefully.

"Is the situation different today? I doubt it. Politicians make promises. Commentators and columnists are ready with quick solutions to complex problems. Gurus are always available to introduce us to new kinds of deities.

"Eli's counsel is therefore still valuable. He told Samuel to pause and hear what God has to say. This is in essence what the University would like you to do also. We are trying to tell every student: 'Withdraw now and then in quiet meditation and worship. Let your soul be attuned to the message of God's Holy Spirit. There are many things to be learned for your life which only the Lord can teach.'

"With a listening heart you can discover for yourself the profound meaning of God's love. You can hear how the Father's mercy was far greater than human sin and short-coming. You can perceive in the Cross of Christ the sign of comfort, hope, and newness of living.

"In this Bicentennial year of the nation we are beginning to realize that our society is adrift, like a great ship without a rudder. Revelations about political chicanery, illegal acts of the CIA, and bribery by multi-national corporations indicate the disintegration of ethical assumptions in our midst. The major professions are becoming alarmed about the disregard for moral obligations which should hold our social structure together.

"The solution does not lie in more laws. It rests in the kind of value systems we set for ourselves. We have opportunity here to make clear what God expects and the priorities which should govern lives. We know that we can have His guidance in sorting out the alternatives. If our efforts falter, we can count on His strength to support us.

"The concept of service is always associated with those who listen to the Lord. Jesus set the ultimate example: 'The Son of Man came not to be served but to serve.' The obligation of a university like ours is to encourage both the motivation and the means of service. Recall how Jesus tested the love of His followers. Did they feed the hungry? Give drink to the thirsty? Take care of those in need?

"The campus is a good place to practice that concern. A listening heart is more than a sympathetic heart. It responds to God's love with readiness to put other people ahead of ourselves. One of the most important lessons we can teach at this University is contained in St. John's admonition: 'This is how we know what love is: Christ gave His life for us. We, too, then, ought to give our lives for our brothers! ...Our love should not be just words and talk; it must be true love, which shows itself in action.'

"The whole point of education is the acquisition of wisdom—not only that which is earthbound, but that which is from above, which the Apostle James says is 'pure, peace-loving, considerate, open to reason...straight-forward and sincere, rich in mercy and in the kindly deeds that are truth.'

"May God grant us all that kind of wisdom. It endures through time and lasts into eternity."

Albert G. Huegli
February 1, 1976

Where are We Going?
Pentecost 21, 1975

Matthew 22:1-14

"As in other of his parables, so here in this one Jesus tells a most improbable tale. A king gives a marriage feast for his son, and invites his guests—only to have them refuse to enter into the nuptial festivities. Who would refuse a king's invitation, a chance to enter the royal palace and for a time take part in the sumptuous splendor that befits the regal heir? Who in his right mind would make light of it, treat it as an ordinary event, and go on with business as usual? Who would maltreat, even kill, the King's heralds announcing the banquet, and risk kingly retaliation? A most improbable story!

"Yet it is only with such an improbable tale that Jesus can describe the improbable events that he has set in motion. The God of Israel sends His Son to His chosen people, through him invites them into His Kingdom—and they say no to Jesus. And thereby they say no to God, to God who has moved a whole series of O.T. promises in his direction. St. John put it very succinctly. He came to his own, and his own received him not. Jesus weeps over the city of Jerusalem, and the king in His anger destroys the city.

"But then the really improbable thing happens. God then sends his servants out into the highways and by-ways to invite the most motley crowd of ragtag have-nots into the wedding banquet. And here we are, beneficiaries all of a surprising turn of events. Gentiles like you and me are recipients of the blessings of the God of Abraham and Isaac and Jacob.

"Whatever else these improbabilities say to us, there is at least one thing that the parable ought not to say. It ought not to be used to nourish among us any unseemly anti-Semitism. Some things are a matter of historical record: Judaism rejects Jesus and his claims, and that has been the case since the very beginning. But that no more authorizes a Christian hatred of the Jews than the early Roman persecution of Christians would justify an anti-Italian movement among Christians.

"The parable does make it clear, however, that God measures our attitude toward Him by our acceptance or rejection of His Son. And that brings us to the point of this story. We are the Johnny-come-latelys in the kingdom of Heaven. St. Paul puts it this way: the Jew first and then the Gentile. And if God did not spare those early Jesus-rejecters, then we may be certain that we also dare not presume upon his goodness. We too ought to be warned not to treat His call lightly, nor to hold in contempt the Beloved Son in whom God is well pleased. That is the message to the sequel to the parable, when the King mingles with the guests at His Son's marriage, and evicts the man who sits there unworthily, wears no wedding garment and thereby snubs the King's generosity. Let not Valpo Christians be numbered among those who take God and His goodness for granted, nor let us be content to observe others hold Christ in contempt.

"Let me suggest a specific area where such admonition may be in place. This fall we are observing the 50th anniversary of Valpo as a Lutheran University. We have been hearing—and shall continue to hear—about the old-timers, about their vision, about their dedication to bring about what we are today at V.U. We owe them a great debt of gratitude, a debt that is only partially discharged by turning the side aisles of the Chapel into a temporary VU hall of fame. We honor our forebears here much more appropriately as we bend our effort to see VU as they saw it—and to that end our Gospel is a great help. It is a kingdom parable, a story of how God runs his affairs. Fifty years ago God invited us to the marriage of His Son, saying: Lutherans, bring your scholars to my marriage feast and let them honor my Son. And let such Christ confessing scholars teach and educate unnumbered generations of students how to love Me, the Lord, their God, with heart and soul and mind. Let such a University under the Cross, teachers and students and administration and staff, let it struggle in its effort to take every thought captive to the obedience of Christ. Come Valpo, come to the marriage feast of the Son.

"Like the old-timers we too must be impressed with the improbabilities contained in such a call. How can a university be Lutheran? What does that even begin to mean? When God conducts His affairs, sends out His call and extends His invitations, improbabilities proliferate. And so do the excuses. And the temptations to disobedience.

"We dare not make light of God's call to the marriage. Our educational program and our efforts at scholarship are invited guests at the banquet of God's Son. It may feel awkward to sit in such splendor. It may irritate to serve the least of Christ's brethren. It may even hurt to follow Christ with His Cross on our back. But we may not pursue business as usual; that luxury is not ours. Once God has called there are only two alternatives. If we would avoid the outer darkness where there is only weeping and gnashing of teeth, the outer darkness of regret, remorse, and recrimination, then we shall have to put on the wedding garment of faith, faith which confidently exults: In thy light we shall see light. Amen."

Walter E. Keller

What is Security?
Pentecost 25, 1980

Luke 20:27-40

"Jesus calls those who are heaven-bound sons of God. Sons and daughters—children of God, part of Abba's family. So you are now and will be in the life to come. That's the first and most important thing you need to know. You can be secure in your trust that a loving and tender Father-God holds you, feeds you and forgives you—all the time—and without conditions. That promise sustains us now. It will sustain us in our dying. And it will sustain us in the life to come.

"A child secure in the loving arms of a parent is able to face tremendous uncertainties in the future. Consider the adjustments a child makes in the first years of life. Fantastic changes occur between the first and second year of life over which the infant has little control, being almost totally dependent on the care and direction of others. The uncertainties are manageable and anticipation of the future is bright if the infant's trust in the promise of his parents is sure.

"So it is when we anticipate our dying and the life which lies beyond that dying. That prospect is very frightening to most people, especially to young people who have so much of life lying ahead of them. If you're not down in the pit of despair because of illness or some monumental personal problem, it's hard to imagine life as better than it is right now? But heavenly life is such an abstract concept, not rooted in any concrete experience. We just don't have many stories coming from the other side of the grave, and even if someone did come back with some glowing tales about life beyond, it's not likely that we'd believe them anyway. So we figure a bird in the hand is worth two in the bush. I'll take my chances with what I've got right here, even if there are a few things I'd like to change. And that makes sense on the basis of what we can know from our present experience and reasoning capacity.

"In the face of our fears about dying and the paucity of our experience and knowledge about what life beyond death might be like, we need to fall back, regress if you will, to the child-like trust of a small child. Luther takes us back to the very beginning of life by comparing the process of dying to the process of birth. Just as an infant moves with peril and pain from the small abode of its mother's womb into the immensity of life on this huge planet, so we must depart this life through the narrow gate of death. And though the world we live in seems very big to us, it is much smaller than the mother's womb in comparison with the future heaven that will be our home. That's why the feast days of saints, in calendar time the day of their death, is known in Latin as Natale, the day of their birth. The narrow passage of death makes us think of this life as expansive and the life beyond as confined because it is difficult for us to see beyond the narrow passage.

"It takes a great deal of trust to face the constrictions which are a part of our dying and the paucity of our imagining what lies beyond the coldness and stillness of the grave. It takes trust in the promise of a God who says to Moses, 'I am the God of your father, the God of Abraham, the God of Isaac, the God of Jacob.' You may regard your ancestors as dead, Moses, and so they are in terms of your experience, alive only in memory, and memory always fades. But I am their God—right now. So, Jesus comments, he is not a God of the dead, but of the living; for all live to him. While death is experienced as a break in the continuity of our relationship to those we love, there is no such break in the continuity of our relationship to God. Our relationship to God does not go through the narrows, which is the literal meaning of the term anxiety, but is rather broadened and deepened as we come to see what now appears only through a glass darkly.

"We cling to the promise as we deal with our anxieties—or better, we hold on to our Father who makes the promise, our Father who is God of the living. And if we feel his everlasting arms securely around us, then we can approach the narrow gate of death with greater anticipation and more excitement than we might guess. For we are sons and daughters of the resurrection, and what God has in store for us is larger and greater than we could hope."

Thomas Droege

Why do We Serve?

Pentecost 17, 1982

Mark 8:27-35

"Jesus clearly understood what the Father had in mind: He was sent here not to condemn the world, but through him the world might be saved. That called for a special kind of commitment. Jesus says in effect: 'I utterly commit myself as a devoted disciple of God. I absorb everything he teaches; and he has equipped me to sustain with a word every one who is wearied. Nothing can divert me from serving. These people may pull the hairs from my beard, they may spit in my face, they may tear the flesh of my back raw with their whips, but my face is set like flint; I will not swerve from my calling. I will persevere.'

"Do you recall how frightened and despondent and full of doubt the disciples were on Easter morning? That suggests that they hadn't listened to all of Christ's prediction, 'I will rise again.' Or at least they hadn't paid attention to those words. It's as if hearing about the crucifixion was so appalling that they could not hear anything else. But the promise of the resurrection is the hope-filled climax of it all. We have a Christ who lives, who is with us, to forgive us, to stand with us when our aims and motives and perspectives are diverted from where our Lord would have us be—and from what he would have us do.

"We often call ourselves here a University under the cross. In doing so, we concede our need to come to the foot of the cross, to look up and remember that our God who knows well how confused we get in our values, and how frustrated and tired we get, how lonesome and helpless we can feel, has forgiveness and love and strength for us. It is he who invites us back 'home,' to take our place at the table-under the cross. It was from the cross that Jesus said to Mary, 'Look at lonely John over there. Treat him as your son—as family.' Then, turning to John he said, 'Look at troubled Mary over there—see her as your very own mother. Care for her. She's family.'

Today, when you take the supper, look across to see your brothers and sisters at the table and remember those whom you don't see but whom Jesus wants for family. Set your faces like flint and say, 'Lord, I believe; forgive my unbelief! God, give me power to seek first of all—more than anything in my life—to love you. I know that means doing what pleases you. And I know finding and caring for troubled people pleases you. And I know that mere saying, 'I love you,' when I do not demonstrate my love in caring for others, is hollow and empty and dead.'

"I do not suggest you drop out of school or that we quit our jobs. But when we study and when we work and when we endeavor to develop our lives and strive to improve to 'become all we can be,' we do so with a commitment to do a better job of serving and loving our neighbor for Christ's sake. And, no matter how difficult this may get we resolutely determine not to be diverted from following our Lord in his mission of conveying his life-giving love to all people.

"Christ has forgiveness for us—because of his cross—for the many times we've been less than faithful, less than forgiving. And he promises strength and his presence as we recommit ourselves to follow him faithfully.

"Now we may be ready to pray together with fervor and understanding the collect we prayed earlier in the service, but might not have fully understood or carefully heard:

> "'O GOD, YOU DECLARE YOUR ALMIGHTY POWER CHIEFLY IN SHOWING MERCY AND PITY, GRANT US THE FULLNESS OF YOUR GRACE, THAT PURSUING WHAT YOU HAVE PROMISED, WE MAY SHARE YOUR HEAVENLY GLORY, THROUGH JESUS CHRIST OUR LORD.' AMEN."

Karl Lutze

Who Loves Me?

"To cross the gulf from Life Alone to Life Beloved—truly to be real, truly to be worthy in the eyes of another—means that you are no more your own possession. You give yourself away, and then games all come to an end. No longer can you pretend excuses or accusations against the world; nor can you imagine lies concerning your beauty, your gifts and possibilities. Everything becomes what it really is, for you are seen and you know it. 'How are you' triggers 'Who are you.' And it wasn't so much that I said it, but rather that I meant it and that I awaited an answer, too—this caused the lonely She to know her loneliness, even in the moment when I offered you the other thing: friendship.

"It's frightening, isn't it?

"To be loved, dear lady, you must let all illusions die. And since, between the bathroom and the kitchen, between People magazine and the Harlequin, your Self was mostly illusion—at least the acceptable self—then to be loved meant that your very Self had to die—at least the acceptable self.

"A rich young ruler came to Jesus, desiring eternal life. He announced that he had kept all the commandments and wondered whether that weren't enough. But Jesus told him he lacked one thing. He ought, said Jesus, to sell all that he had and give the money to the poor. Upon these words, two were made sorrowful: the rich, because he could not lose his riches, which were his identity and his Self; he turned away. And Jesus, because he loved and would not love this man; but the man turned away.

"Riches. O my dear and lonely lady, how rich are you in your illusions. Ironically, you cling to the very loneliness which you despise. It feels safe. But love—God's love—always comes in light. That's what scares you. Light illumines truth: obesity, the foolish game between Ayds and potato chips, between cigarettes and vitamins. These things are the truth. These you bide. Yet it is only truth that Jesus can love. He cannot love your imaginings, your riches. Sell all that you have. Undress—

"Not me, after all. It is Jesus who asks, 'How are you?' And if you would then sell the false self by which you sustain the contemptible Self and die; if you would answer truly, 'I'm fat, helpless and alone, unlovely,' then he would love you. No: then you would know that he has loved you all along. To see one truth is to discover the other—which is that he loves you not because you are lovable, but because he is love. And here is the power of his love, that it makes ugliness beautiful! To be loved of God is to be lovely indeed.

"All night long I ask, 'How are you?' I can't sleep, waiting for the truth: 'I'm just terrible.' For then I would cry, 'Good! Now there's a confession I can love!'

"And the mighty God, the trumpet-voiced, cries, 'I love a child. But she is afraid of me. Then how can I come to her, to feed and to heal her by my love?'"

Walter Wangerin, Jr.

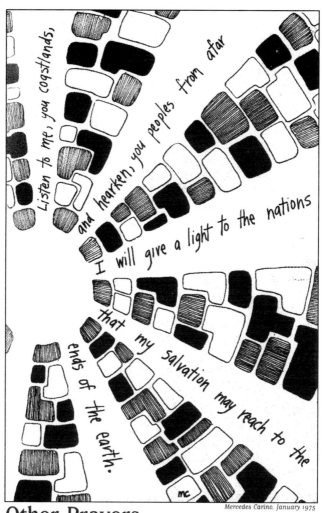

Listen to me, you coastlands,
and hearken, you peoples from afar
I will give a light to the nations
that my salvation may reach to the
ends of the earth.

mc

Mercedes Carino, January 1975

Other Prayers
for Daily Life

Other Prayers for Daily Life

Prayers for Many Moments

Open my hands (a prayer for times of change)

"Suddenly the years
are going by too quickly.
Father, help me to understand
the changes that will come
and to accept.
Help me to cooperate with You.

Open my hands!
Let me learn
to hold the years with open hands,
carefully savoring each pain, each joy;
gently holding each love,
remembering Your mercy of yesterday
and reaching out
to take gifts
You will offer me tomorrow."

Anne Zink Springsteen

For Monday morning

Lord God, thank you for the weekend, which I enjoyed
having—even though it seems now too short. What did you
do after your Sabbath day rest? There are lots of things
ahead of me this week, and I probably won't accomplish all
of them. Be with me and keep me on task, grateful to have
work that I like, and filled with energy to do it. Amen.

For Wednesday

I'm not sure that this week is ever going to end, Lord, and
you know where I need help most. Bring me your strength
to keep working calmly at the things I can do; help me let
go of the things I can't do anything about. One day at a
time, Lord. Amen.

For Friday afternoon

There were times, Lord, when I didn't think I'd make it, but here I am ready to start the weekend. I'm tired, but excited about plans for relaxing, for time with friends, for special occasions coming up. Keep me safe, help me to behave in ways that make me and others stronger. Help me to avoid the temptation to skip the observance of Your day on Sunday morning. I want You to be part of these times of rest and play, just like You are part of the working times. Amen.

When going to bed

Dear Lord, I wish that I had the discipline to pray with real energy and devotion every night, and I ask that You will help to guide me toward this as I get older. But just tonight, as I'm falling asleep, thank You for the feeling that I am resting safely in Your care. Bless those I love, hold the world in security, and give us tomorrow a new day in which to accomplish Your will. Amen.

When things are going well

Everything in my life is working out just right at the moment, and I want to say, "Thanks!" It feels good! I know I usually turn to my prayers more quickly when I'm in trouble, but let me remember that You are my God when I am doing well. The world actually feels grace-filled to me—like sunshine pouring through a clean window—and I'm grateful. Spread this around, Lord, so that others also can sense Your blessings in their lives. Amen.

When something wonderful has happened

Thank you, Lord, for the special and wonderful blessing in my life today. It's what I wanted, but I hardly dared believe that I would get it. I want to jump up and down and yell, but that would be bragging, and would make me look silly, but it would be just right. Have You got some better idea for how I could let others know my happiness? I'm listening. Amen.

When choosing between many opportunities

God, there are so many opportunities to become involved here in the campus community. Sometimes it's overwhelming, but I feel so good when I'm doing fun stuff and helping people out. And besides all the academics and the friends I've made, there's also this feeling of getting closer to You. As time rolls on, I hope I can find time to take a break from my busy schedule and spend at least a few moments praying or just sitting quietly. Thanks for Your presence in my life, Lord. In Christ's name. Amen.

For a troubled relationship

Lord, you promise to be there in every part of my life, and I know that I need you now. I want this relationship to be perfect, but it's way out of control. I feel anxious, guilty, and stressed out all the time. I don't think that it can be right to be so worried about everything—am I giving in too much? Am I being too stubborn? Am I hovering and bothering? Or am I ignoring that person's needs as much as she/he claims I am? Why didn't You give really specific instructions for how to love another person well? Help me find some way to understand this puzzle that, according to movies and songs, ought to be easy. Amen.

For problems with enemies

Maybe I'm over-reacting, Lord, but I am sure that there is a person who just wants me to hurt. Even when I try, I see this person as a real nuisance, an obstacle to me in every way. I wish we were on opposite sides of the planet! But certainly one classroom, one office, one residence hall is too small for both of us! Do something! I'm tired of struggling with this person, and tired of struggling with my own feelings of anger and bitterness. Lord, help me to turn this situation, or at least my attitude, around. Amen.

For family struggles

Dear Lord, I know I've read somewhere that it was Your good plan to put people into families. But this week, I've really felt burdened by the troubles and struggles of my family. I know they all need Your blessing, Lord, but I need a little space. I need to see that I cannot fix everything that is wrong at home, and that You will be with me—and with them—even if we're apart. Amen.

When I seem to have lost focus

No matter how hard I try today, dear God, I cannot remember what I've read, and my thinking flies in all directions. Perhaps this comes from sheer weariness. But maybe I've lost a sense of direction, too. Things don't sink in because I've no clue what I'll ever use them for. Help me, Lord, to discern the useful service toward which I may point my life and energy. Then strengthen me to put my whole self into the effort of becoming someone who will accomplish Your purposes on this earth. In Jesus' name I pray. Amen.

Thanks for the beauty of God's creation

In this summer season, I love having the time to be outside and notice the details around me. My own corner of the world may not rank on the list of the World's Most Beautiful, but it is beautiful to me when I stop to experience it. Remind me often of this beauty, and help me to have the energy to preserve it in every way I can. Your gift should be something I care for and care about. In Christ's name. Amen.

Thanks for bodily strength

Lord, you are sometimes described as energy itself, and there are times when I feel that energy as part of my own, and sense a thrill in being close to You. I am grateful for the strength of my body, and I want to preserve it and make it a good instrument for You and for others. Help me to be patient with those who don't know You this way. Keep me strong and healthy, increase my stamina, give me the will power to avoid anything what would make my body less than it can be. Amen.

Thanks for my family life

Lord God, you have given me a great gift by putting me into this family. Today I realize what a blessing this is! After all, I could have been anybody's child, but I have these terrific parents and these specifically weird and wonderful sibs. We have our own special routines and rituals—and these make me feel secure and happy. Give me the memory of these feelings when my family ties seem burdensome and problematic. Amen.

This quiet night (a bedtime prayer)

"Life has come to a close, Father.
I will sleep and be as close to death
as I will ever willingly come.
This day of grace has ended,
and I know only a very little
about what it all may mean
for tomorrow or next year.
But You have been with me in everything.
Now I put this day aside,
with everything that happened
wrapped in Your forgiveness.
Whatever this day will become
for me and others
I put in your hands."

Anne Zink Springsteen

Classic Christian Prayers

Purity of heart

"Almighty God, in whom we live and move and have our being, you have made us for yourself and our hearts are restless until they find their rest in you. Grant us purity of heart and strength of purpose, that no selfish passion may hinder us from knowing your will, no weakness from doing it; but that in your light we may see light clearly, and in your service we may find our perfect freedom; through Jesus Christ our Lord. Amen."

Augustine, Bishop of Hippo (364)

A Prayer of St. Francis

"Lord, make me an instrument of your peace.
Where there is hatred, let me sow love, where there is injury, pardon, where there is doubt, faith, where there is despair, hope, where there is darkness, light, where there is sadness, joy.

O Divine Master, grant that we may not so much seek to be consoled as to console, not so much to be understood as to understand, not so much to be loved as to love. For it is in giving that we receive, it is in pardoning that we are pardoned, it is in dying that we are born to eternal life. Amen."

St Francis of Assisi

The Serenity Prayer

"God, give us the serenity to accept what cannot be changed; give us the courage to change what should be changed; give us the wisdom to distinguish one from the other. Amen."

Reinhold Niebuhr

Vocation

"Keep us, Lord, so awake in the duties of our callings that we may sleep in your peace and wake in your glory. Amen."

John Donne

Martin Luther's morning prayer

We give thanks to you, heavenly Father, through Jesus
Christ your dear Son, that you have protected us through
the night from all danger and harm; and we beseech you
to preserve and keep us, this day also, from all sin and
evil; that in all our thoughts, words an deeds, we may
serve and please you. Into your hands we commend our
bodies and souls, and all that is ours. Let your holy
angel guard us, that the wicked one may have no power
over us. Amen.

Martin Luther's evening prayer

I thank you, my heavenly Father, through Jesus Christ, your
dear Son, that you have graciously kept me this day; and I
pray you that you would forgive me all my sins where I
have done wrong, and graciously keep me this night. For
into your hands I commend myself, my body and soul, and
all things. Let your holy angel be with me, that the wicked
one may have no power over me. Amen.

Renewal of vocation

"O Lord, renew our spirits and draw our hearts to yourself,
that our work may not be to us a burden but a delight. Let
us not serve you with the spirit of bondage like slaves, but
with freedom and gladness, delighting in you and rejoicing
in your work, for Jesus Christ's sake. Amen."

Benjamin Jenks

In times of stress

"Blessed Jesus, you are always near in times of stress.
Although we cannot feel your presence you are close.
You are always there to help and watch over us.
Nothing in heaven or on earth can separate you from us.
Amen."

Margery Kempe, 15th century

In time of difficulty

IN YOU, O LORD, I SEEK REFUGE;
DO NOT LET ME EVER BE PUT TO SHAME;
IN YOUR RIGHTEOUSNESS DELIVER ME.
INCLINE YOUR EAR TO ME;
RESCUE ME SPEEDILY.
BE A ROCK OF REFUGE FOR ME,
A STRONG FORTRESS TO SAVE ME.
INTO YOUR HAND I COMMIT MY SPIRIT;
YOU HAVE REDEEMED ME, O LORD, FAITHFUL GOD.

Psalm 31:1-2, 5

In time of illness

"O Lord God of our salvation, to whom no sickness is
incurable, we pray that in your compassion you will drive
away from your servants who look for your heavenly
medicine, all illness; show forth in them the might of your
healing power, and make them whole both in body and
soul; through Jesus Christ our Lord. Amen."

Mozarabic Psalter

Approaching death

"Finish, then, Thy new creation;
Pure and spotless let us be.
Let us see Thy great salvation
Perfectly restored in Thee;
Changed from glory into glory,
Till in heaven we take our place,
Till we cast our crowns before Thee,
Lost in wonder, love, and praise. Amen."

Charles Wesley

At the opening of a meeting

Heavenly Father, as we meet now in your presence,
we ask you to open our ears to hear your voice,
to open our lips to sing your praise,
and to open our hearts to love you more and more;
for Christ our Savior's sake. Amen.

At the close of a meeting or worship

Heavenly Father, be pleased to accept and bless all that we
have offered to you in this act of worship; and give us
grace to show your praise not only with our lips, but in
our lives; through Jesus Christ our Lord. Amen.

Before receiving the Lord's Supper

"Almighty God, unto whom all hearts be open, and all
desires known, and from whom no secrets are hid: cleanse
the thoughts of our hearts by the inspiration of thy Holy
Spirit: that we may perfectly love thee, and worthily
magnify thy holy name: through Christ our Lord. Amen."

Book of Common Prayer, 1549

After receiving the Lord's Supper

"We give thanks to you, almighty God, that you have
refreshed us with this salutary gift; and we pray that in
your mercy you will strengthen our faith in you, and in
fervent love toward one another; through Jesus Christ, your
dear Son, our Lord, who lives and reigns with you and the
Holy Spirit, ever one God, world without end. Amen."

Martin Luther